Institutionalization
of Usability

Institutionalization of Usability

A Step-by-Step Guide

Eric Schaffer

✦✦Addison-Wesley

Boston • San Francisco • New York • Toronto • Montreal
London • Munich • Paris • Madrid
Capetown • Sydney • Tokyo • Singapore • Mexico City

The publisher offers discounts on this book when ordered in quantity bulk purchases and special sales. For more information, please contact:

> U.S. Corporate and Government Sales
> (800) 382-3419
> corpsales@pearsontechgroup.com

For sales outside of the U.S., please contact:

> International Sales
> (317) 581-3793
> international@pearsontechgroup.com

Visit Addison-Wesley on the Web: www.awprofessional.com

Library of Congress Cataloging-in-Publication Data

CIP data on file.

ISBN: 0-321-17934-X
Text printed on recycled paper
1 2 3 4 5 6 7 8 9 10—CRS—0807060504
First printing, February 2004

Contents

Preface

This book is a guide to making usability a routine practice within an enterprise, be it commercial or government. Every organization has special needs: There is no one simple approach that fits all organizations. What this book provides, however, is a solid methodology, not for usability engineering (that's been done before and exists in various forms), but for the part that is truly missing—the institutionalization of usability. This institutionalization methodology is not new. It is simply a synthesis of the best practices and insights from hundreds of companies in the forefront of this effort. This book will give you insights into the appropriate institutionalization activities, infrastructure, and staffing. It will give you tips on how to recognize quality, and how to time and sequence components. The combination of elements is unique for each organization, but this book can be a road map, a mine detector, and a shopping list for you.

There is a misconception that the institutionalization of usability will simply be a matter of doing more of what we have done in the past. A simple analogy will illustrate why this is a misconception. Imagine that we are back in pre-industrial times and that we have a small hut in the forest where we have made a primitive brick forge to produce swords. We create the swords by using a hand bellows and then hammering the metal against a rock. We find the swords to be very useful and realize we need one for everyone in our army. We need thousands of swords. Is our solution to build lots of little huts? Of course not. We need a factory.

Today, the usability engineering process is still being done in a hut. Usability engineers are typically thrown alone into a large organization and left unsupported. There is no established user-centric methodology or set of tools. Every questionnaire is reinvented from scratch. Every deliverable is conceived and crafted by hand. Then we wonder why user-centered design can seem inefficient! It should be no surprise if the results are not consistent, not repeatable, and not reliable.

Currently, good usability practitioners know how to make software usable. We have a billion dollars worth of research and 50 years of practice. But, the usability industry has not matured nearly as much as the software development industry. Usability professionals rarely complete a systematic and repeatable methodology. They rarely work with a complete toolset and set of standards. They are rarely formally trained to complete all the tasks in their area of responsibility. They rarely have comprehensive quality assurance. And perhaps of greatest concern, they are rarely integrated into the routine development process. We know how to make an application usable, but we don't generally know how to put these techniques into practice in a systematic way that is efficient and works well within an organization.

This is the next frontier in the usability field and it is also the focus of this book. This book provides insights into the deep changes necessary to put user-centered design to work routinely within your organization. This book also provides a guided series of activities and milestones that will chart your course to fully mature and institutionalized usability engineering.

This book is about how to create a usability "factory." It is about how to create a reliable and repeatable process. It is about how to ensure efficiency. Following this process means that usability efforts will have to be done differently than before. Just as a computer programmer would never suggest going back to the early days "in the garage," no usability expert should accept the lack of a systematic methodology and professional infrastructure. Usability practitioners of the future will look back with amusement at our current piecemeal approach. This book is a guide to this more mature usability engineering process.

It is time for us to get serious about the institutionalization of usability because usability has become extremely important. Usability is now *the* key differentiator in the information age. Imagine the CEO of a large insurance company standing before her stockholders and telling them there is bad news this year. The company has been vanquished by the competition . . . because the competition has better laptop computers. Seems like an unlikely excuse? That's because hardware is now a commodity. It takes serious work to create good hardware, but everyone has it, and it does not represent a differentiator between companies. You just buy adequate hardware.

Hardware was the first wave of the information age. In the 1980s, it was a challenge to get adequate hardware, and it was an important differentiator that could determine corporate success. But at the end of the 1980s, the software industry realized that "software sells the hardware," and good software became the differentiator. Companies who could create stable software with the right functionality won big. This was the second wave.

Now in the new millennium, software has become a commodity. Everyone can create a database. Everyone can get connectivity. Children can code in HTML. Software is no longer a differentiator. Software coding is being done with better and better power tools and being outsourced to countries with lower labor costs. We are now entering the third wave of the information age.

What is the remaining differentiator in this information age? It is the ability to build *practical, useful, usable, and satisfying* applications and web sites. Very few companies do this well, because this requires creating a full and integrated usability engineering capability. As you will see throughout this book, the journey to routine usability requires a serious effort and the path has many pitfalls.

The Organization of This Book

This book contains four major sections, or *phases*. The first phase, "Startup," covers the process of alerting the organization to the need to make usability a routine internal capability. It then outlines the steps toward finding an executive champion and consultant to support the initial process.

The "Setup" phase explores the essential core infrastructure of methods, templates, standards, and internal training.

"Organization," the third phase, describes the need to properly staff the factory you have built. You will need a small, centralized, internal organization to support usability engineering. If you are a large organization, you will need usability practitioners reporting within your project teams. The Organization phase then ends by outlining the importance of applying your usability methods to a set of projects and discussing challenges that occur as resources are stretched (as often happens at this point).

The last phase, "Long-Term Operations," characterizes the established operation of the central usability group.

The Audience for This Book

This book enables leaders to bring modern usability principles into everyday practice. It is not an introduction to usability or a guide to good design. This book is for everyone who is working to integrate usability-engineering practices into their organizations.

If you are an executive or manager within an organization, then you will want to focus on the steps you can take to get institutionalization started. You will want to concentrate on a high-level strategy, and deciding on the staff and resources to fully implement the institutionalization process. Pay particular attention to the chapters on being an executive champion and creating a strategy. You are the one who must move your organization from piecemeal usability to a managed process.

If you are currently part of a usability team that is struggling to make usability routine, you may need to look at the process of institutionalization in a new light. Perhaps you are struggling because you can't do it alone. You may need to focus on finding an executive champion to give power to the effort.

If you are part of a large organization, all the steps in the institutionalization method will be critical, and you will likely have to involve many others along the way. If you are with a small or medium size organization, then you may be able to do much of this on your own.

The steps will still be appropriate for you, even if they are scaled down.

No matter who you are, or how far along you are in the institution-alization process (even if it is at the beginning), if you are consider-ing how to institutionalize usability in your company, this book is for you. If you have decided to proceed to build usability into your software design practices, this book is required reading. Whether you are an executive leading the process, a manager supporting the transition, or a staff member advising others and working on usabil-ity issues, this book will guide you to success.

Acknowledgments

This book was drafted from my personal experience with thousands of individuals who, over the last quarter century, have struggled to instill usability engineering capabilities within their companies. While I cannot possibly name them all, I am sure they will see themselves within these pages, sharing their insights and knowledge through my eyes. This book is theirs more than mine.

I would like to thank Dr. Robert Bailey, Dr. Darryl Yoblick, and Gary Griggs, who were my mentors when I first joined the field. Without them I don't know if I *ever* would have figured out how to do this work right. I would also like to thank the pioneers of institutionalization who created effective usability departments. Among these, special thanks to Dr. Arnie Lund, Dr. Ed Israelski, and Dr. Tom Tullis, from whom I learned much.

I would like to thank the staff at Human Factors International, Inc. (HFI). Our president, Jay More, has been at my side for nearly 15 years, helping me to see usability from a business perspective. I am indebted to Apala Lahiri Chavan, Dr. Phil Goddard, Dr. Susan Weinschenk, and Dr. Kath Straub for their technical contributions and review of this book. Indeed, my entire staff at HFI has contributed in so many ways to this book, developing methods, sharing ideas, and working directly on the book itself.

I would like to thank the pioneering clients I have been able to work with in applying institutionalization strategies. In particular, thanks to Carolyn Burke and Nicole Poirier from the RBC Royal Bank in Canada. And a note of thanks to my editor at Addison-Wesley, Peter Gordon, who saw what was possible from our early outlines, and provided invaluable counsel and support.

While there have been many who have given me ideas and comments, I am especially thankful for my colleagues who took the time to contribute their insights and advice to the readers directly, particularly:

Aaron Marcus, President, Aaron Marcus and Associates

Apala Lahiri Chavan, Managing Director, Human Factors International—India

Arnie Lund, Director of Design and Usability, Microsoft

Colin Hynes, Director of Site Usability, Staples

Dana Griffith, CUA, Web Consultant, Interactive Media, American Electric Power

Ed Israelski, Program Manager—Human Factors, Abbott Laboratories

Harley Manning, Research Director, Forrester Research

Janice Nall, Web Chief Manager, Communication Technologies Branch, National Cancer Institute

Feliça Selenko, Principal Technical Staff Member, AT&T

Pat Malecek, CUA, User Experience Manager, A.G. Edwards & Sons, Inc.

Phil Goddard, Director of Training and Certification, Human Factors International

Sean Wheeler, Lead Usability Specialist, The Social Security Administration

Todd Gross, Director, Corporate Statistics/Human Factors, Medtronic MiniMed

Finally, my special thanks to Bryan Floyd, who is vice president of marketing at HFI. He always believed in me, in my vision, and in our ability to share it with the world. He and his staff worked long and hard to help assemble and edit this book. Maura Gibbons Vij was the primary coordinator of this effort and without her patient coordination, review, editing, research, and attention to detail, this book would not have been possible. Also, my thanks to Rebecca Greenberg, who provided outstanding restructuring, rewriting, and refinement to the early draft of this book, and to Riya Thosar, Doug Walker, Ulhas Moses, and Ashwini Garde, who provided or refined the graphics in this book.

Chapter 1

The Deep Changes

> ➤ Change your organization's focus from building lots of functions to meeting user needs.
>
> ➤ Change your organization's focus from developing cool and impressive technology to creating software that is simple, practical, and useful.
>
> ➤ Help executives and project managers focus on the value of usability.
>
> ➤ Customize and follow a systematic and complete process for institutionalizing usability.

You are embarking on a program to institutionalize usability in your organization. What is the long-term view? You may find that your company already has some of the organization or groundwork in place, and you may be well on your way to establishing a user-centered process. This book can help you get there. If you are starting from scratch, it may take almost two years before the full implementation is in place and usability has become a routine practice. However, significant benefits and progress will occur before then, and you'll recognize and appreciate gains as you work toward full implementation.

1

Of course, there may be some setbacks along the way. These almost always come in the areas of mindset, relationships, and communication. These setbacks will illuminate the deep issues that you must work on continuously. These issues are explored in the first chapter of this book and *not* fully covered in the following chapters that explore infrastructure components, staffing requirements, and activities because they transcend the surface level. Addressing these issues involves shifting the core belief system of your organization, and that is why they are so important to consider early in the process.

There is a large natural disconnect between the viewpoint of the usability staff and that of the development team. It's not unusual to experience some conflict and misunderstanding. People are attached to their designs, so criticism creates hard feelings. People are also attached to design decisions (like the use of drop-down menus as a solution to all navigation). People see the world in terms of their context, and it is hard to get them to see the user's viewpoint. Once you realize the value of usability engineering, it is difficult to be patient with those who haven't. But ignoring the hard work of shifting others' perspectives makes it likely that all your accomplishments will do little. Good standards and facilities will sit idle if these deeper shifts fail to happen. The following section explores the deep changes that the real institutionalization of usability requires.

Changing the Feature Mindset

A deep philosophical change must take place in the shift to user-centered development. Most companies build applications intent on meeting a given time frame and providing a specific level of functionality. There is a whole flow of feature ideas, but this flow is not really user-centered—it is usually a combination of executive inspiration and customer comments. So how can a selection of features based partly on customer comments and requests not be considered user-centered? Certainly, this type of selection process must involve listening to the user. But often, it only gives the illusion of listening to the user. In many situations, these "customer" requests come from executives, marketing departments, or sales staff. The real user is not studied or fully understood by most of these well-meaning "user representatives." In other situations, comments do flow from actual users. The users send ideas, but typically only very happy or very angry customers send feedback. Also, the comments tend to focus on features, rather than the overall design, error handling, page layout, or other usability issues. The result is the design of features that may not represent the majority of end users and may not address the application as a whole.

It isn't enough to just apply standard usability techniques such as usability testing because just applying techniques does not address the underlying issue. There is still a need to change the focus away from functionality. Software developers often build applications that have unneeded functions, following a checklist of features for each product. Unfortunately, a clutter of irrelevant features contributes to a serious usability problem. The whole focus of the development team is on creating all these functions on time, but if they are not needed or can't be used, is timeliness so important?

It will take some work to get your organization to understand that the function race was one of the roads to success in the 1990s, but it is not so today. Certainly, users want features. Some users focus on attaining the maximum set of features and actually thrive on the challenge of learning their operation, but this is typically a small group of early adopters. In this new millennium, software and Web site developers must deliver adequate features that are simple and useful. Most users want information appliances to be as easy to operate as a toaster—practical, useful, usable, and satisfying solutions. This requires a broader change to the mindset of design and development.

Changing the Technology Mindset

Most people who work in information technology (IT) love the technology. They are in the field because technology is fun, challenging, and impressive. The developer's job is to understand the technology and use it. Therefore, developers naturally focus on learning about the technology, and they feel excited about using the latest, most powerful facility. To a degree, this creates development groups that are more focused on creating something impressive and cool instead of practical and useful.

Knowledge of usability factors, together with working with usability engineers, helps create a major shift in the way that IT professionals see technology. Technology is a tool that lets you meet user needs. Much like a professional carpenter who picks the tool that best meets the need and does not anxiously seek an excuse to use the latest hammer, developers need to focus on creating the right tools and not just the tools they want to create.

The people who have to use the technology may not be using it because it is new and fun. Although there are always early adopters, most technology users want to use the tool to get something done—get information from a Web site, pay their bills online, or look up directions. Most users are not looking for technology that is challenging and interesting. They want the *result* to be useful and interesting. In fact, many users expect the technology to be not challenging but actually transparent. Professional developers are often intrigued by the technology and its quirks. Users often find the quirks annoying.

Changing Management Values

While the development community changes from fixation on features and new technologies, management must also change. Management is used to asking whether milestones and budgets are under control and establishing compensation schemes that reinforce the need to produce functions on schedule. This has worked well in the past, but it won't work well in the future. Things that were thought of as secondary intangibles and "nice-to-haves" must be quantified and managed. They are the key to the future.

Management must understand that the company is building not just systems that will function but also systems that must work in the context of a given range of users, doing a given set of tasks, in a given environment. Success is measured as the real business value of the application. To be a success, it takes much more than just delivering the Web site or application on time. The deliverable must be usable and satisfying to operate. The outcome of the design will depend on the organization and may include increased sales or enrollment, more leads, increased willingness to pay fees, larger sets of items per purchase, and so on. These are the results that usability buys you. Few organizations will not directly benefit from good usability engineering.

Advice for Those Considering an Investment in Usability
By Harley Manning, Research Director, Forrester Research

The single biggest gap in knowledge we see at Forrester is a lack of understanding of *what* and *why*. *What* makes for a great user experience, and *why* you should care—tied to numbers. That's the great barrier. People must understand that there are objective methods of improving user experience and that user experience moves business metrics.

The second biggest gap is a lack of the right skills. We see a hierarchy of skills, process, and organization, where skills are the most important. Whether you try to do this kind of development internally (which is a trend we see) or hire out, you still need somebody on the inside with a deep clue. Otherwise, you're not going to follow the right processes, even if you have them in place, and you're not going to hire the right vendors or manage them effectively.

Regarding processes, there are many good processes out there—just pick one and use it consistently. I was talking with the Web development team at Michelin Tire, and I said, you guys don't wake up in the morning and say, how should we manufacture tires today, do you? And they said, of course not, but we never thought of a Web site that way. They're smart—as soon as I said this, they got it.

Business schools have always taught about marketing issues and brand management, but now they must go further. Marketing can point out a potential market niche; usability engineering can help build a product that will reliably succeed in that niche. The implications of poor usability can be catastrophic for a company. It therefore makes sense that executives and senior management attend to this critical success factor. Project and business line managers are interested in identifiable metrics. As usability matures within an organization, it is not enough to occasionally review the latest "customer satisfaction rating." Depending on the type of Web site or application, executives must be concerned about task speed, task failure rates, drop-off rates, competitive metrics, returns on investment (ROIs), retention rates, and other factors. Executives must be aware of and support a user-centered process. Perhaps most importantly, executives must care about user experience and performance levels as an essential success factor.

Changing the Process for Interface Design

Many companies expect developers to sit down and just draft the interface design without doing expert reviews, data gathering, or any testing. If your organization currently uses this approach, you must be willing to learn and use a different approach. User interface design must be an iterative process. You sketch and prototype an interface, then change it, then get feedback from users, then change it, again and again. There are two reasons why effective interface design must be iterative.

1. Design is a process of deciding among many sets of alternatives. Getting them all correct the first time is virtually impossible.
2. As users see what an interface is actually like, they change their conceptions and expectations—thus the requirements change.

User interface design, by nature, is too complex for anyone to accomplish successfully without feedback. Even usability professionals with decades of experience don't expect to sit down to design a screen and get it right the first time.

Everyone developing software and Web sites needs to remember that both development and design are iterative processes. Being brilliant does help, but the willingness to get feedback and apply it selectively is more important. Designers must be willing to learn and create better designs each time, and organizations need to have a culture that supports such iterations without blame.

Usability within Government

By Janice Nall, Chief, Communication Technologies Branch, National Cancer Institute

There are probably three or four core things we have done to institutionalize usability. Number one is involving the leadership—through presentations and participating in testing or showing them results of a usable site versus a nonusable site.

Number two is using the language from leaders driving the new trend to e-government. Because the National Cancer Institute is part of the government, it helps to be able to tell our leadership that usability and user-centered design are supported, from the President of the United States to the Office of Management and Budget to the Department of Health and Human Services (HHS). Using their own words, language, and documents has been very powerful.

Number three is training, which has been hugely successful—a way to institutionalize usability across HHS and the federal government. We believe in teaching people to fish rather than feeding them the fish. We also use tools and resources, like the Research-Based Web Design and Usability Guidelines, to teach them.

And number four, we have a list of about 500 federal people who receive our online publication *U-Group* (shorthand for *usability group*) via the U-group listserv. Through this listserv, we are trying to get current information out and we're saying, let's share information, let's collaborate—encouraging people to share lessons learned.

The Step-by-Step Process for Institutionalizing Usability

The final deep challenge is the tendency to address usability in a piecemeal fashion. Many companies that see the value of usability still attempt to address it with a series of uncoordinated projects. Instead, there must be a managed usability effort. In this section, I outline the process covered in this book. It is gleaned from experiences of working with hundreds of companies across 20 years within the field of usability at Human Factors International, Inc. (HFI).

Figure 1-1[1] illustrates the typical flow of activities for institutionalizing usability in your organization. You need to make sure these

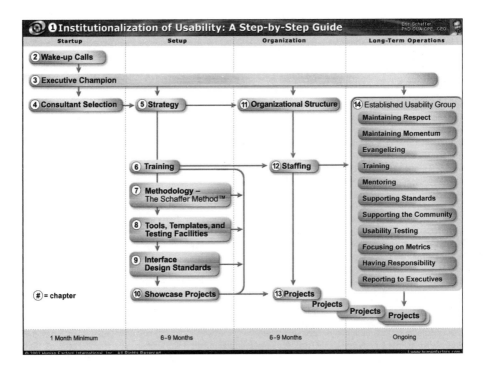

Figure 1-1: *Overview of the Institutionalization of Usability Process*

---

1. We have provided a larger version in the Appendix.

activities fit with your corporate culture and circumstances. In fact, you cannot hope to be successful if you treat this process as you would treat steps within a simple kit. To succeed, you need to proceed consciously and creatively. Since 1981, HFI has worked with many companies and organizations that have not institutionalized usability yet and some who have. Based on thousands of projects and experiences with hundreds of clients, HFI has distilled, tested, and refined the key elements that lead to success. Dozens of companies, large and small, have followed this process and experienced more efficient usability methods and processes as well as more effective products and applications.

The following sections briefly describe each of these phases—Startup, Setup, Organization, and Long-Term Operations. Later chapters discuss each step in detail.

The Startup Phase

It is very rare to find a company that starts out with a focus on usability. Most companies begin with a focus on a business objective (like insurance sales) or on the application of a technology (like handheld devices). That is why there is a need for an initial *wake-up call* on the value of easy-to-use products. The wake-up call can be gentle, such as a key opinion leader becoming inspired while reading an article, or it can be a bit more harsh, such as customers rejecting a new application.

The wake-up call is the impetus to move forward. But the key to early success is the identification of an *executive champion*. This person provides the leadership, resources, and coordination for going forward. This person takes the wake-up call to heart and moves institutionalization forward within the organization.

It is challenging to start a usability institutionalization program from scratch without help from a usability *consultant* who has the training, tools, and an established team. You will also select and train an in-house staff later in the process, but you will need help getting started. Selecting a consultant is important because you need to find a person or company who has the skills and infrastructure to help your organization or the ability to train your staff to complete the activities themselves.

The Setup Phase

You need a *strategy* that fits your organization. The strategy should be specific about what will be done. The strategy should include the timing, sequence, validation, and funding that will be necessary for your usability program to be successful. You may prefer to let the strategy evolve over time, or you can develop an all-encompassing, multiple-year project plan.

The initial strategy for institutionalization of usability should include *training* for in-house staff. You can provide general training for the development community and more extensive training and perhaps certification for those who will be interface development professionals. Out of this training, staff who are talented and interested in the usability field will probably emerge.

Every company has a *methodology* for system development. It may be homegrown or purchased, but in either case, it is unlikely that the existing methodology does a good job of supporting user-centered design. It is important to have a user-centered design method in place, one integrated with current methods and accepted by management and staff. Otherwise, there is no common road map that will pull usability engineering into the design process.

The methodology guides you through a whole set of user-centered design activities, while a training program ensures that you know how to complete them. In addition, there is a whole toolkit of *tools, templates, and testing facilities* that you need to be able to work with effectively. This toolkit should include a venue for testing, templates for questionnaires and deliverables, and usability testing equipment.

Separate from the tools, templates, and testing facilities are the critical *interface design standards*. Standards help both the developers and the usability staff. Even if you had several usability staff members on a project, you would have poor results without standards in place. The experts would each independently design good interfaces, but their designs would be inconsistent and incompatible.

At the end of the Setup phase, it usually makes sense to have one or more *showcase projects*. Conducting these projects provides an opportunity for the training and standards to come together, be shaken out, and be proven. It also offers a chance to share the value of usability with the whole development community.

The Organization Phase

With successful completion of the Setup phase, you have a solid and proven infrastructure for usability work, methods, tools, and standards, as well as a process that works. It remains important to follow the *organizational design* principle of spreading usability throughout your company or agency. Usability should not reside within a single group or team; in order to succeed, usability must permeate the entire organization and become part of the system. In all cases, you need a small, centralized, internal group to support your usability initiatives. For medium- and large-sized companies, usability practitioners need to report to specific project teams. The executive champion needs to establish the right placement and reporting for the group and the practitioners.

This is the appropriate time to start *staffing* the organization. Now the full process of user-centered design is working within your organization, and you can project the best way to put a team into the framework. The steps you went through in the Setup phase provide a clear understanding of the types of people needed.

When establishing a central staff group, most companies use at least some internal staff. In the prior training process, there is a good chance that several people will stand out. This is part of the reason that the internal organization is generally established *after* the training—it provides an opportunity for the internal staff to join the team. It is usually important to hire some additional highly qualified usability staff. In this way, the organization benefits from insiders who know the corporate culture and outsiders who are more knowledgeable about usability technology. A manager of the central usability group should be the main "go to" person for the usability staff.

With the usability staff in place, it is time to apply usability methods to a whole set of *projects*. Doing so gives immediate results and value. It will soon be possible to have every project completed with appropriate user-centered design methods, but in the immediate future you are likely to need to manage a shortage of usability staff. To remedy this and to cost-effectively manage large volumes of usability work, offshore usability teams can be a worthwhile addition to the overall staffing strategy.

The Long-Term Operations Phase

The established *central group* now has an ongoing role in supporting the usability engineering process. This role includes the maintenance of the usability infrastructure and skill sets within the organization. Usability practitioners should now be involved in all development work, following the user-centered methodology and applying the resources established in the Setup phase and continually updated by the central usability team.

As the usability institutionalization effort matures, the relatively informal executive champion may give way (or be promoted) to Chief User Experience Officer (CXO). This is *not* a Chief Usability Officer, but rather a broader role. The CXO is responsible for the overall quality of customer experience. Being a CXO requires expertise in usability as well as a thorough understanding of many other disciplines, including aspects of branding, marketing, graphics, and content development. The CXO must be an officer who can reach across lines of business to ensure compatibility of presentation and messaging. If the role of CXO is not established, the central usability team will have to be placed under some executive organization, like marketing, and the company must ensure that the team members receive good executive stewardship.

In choosing to begin an institutionalization process at your organization, you are choosing to change the feature mindset, technology mindset, management values, and process for interface design that previously governed your operations. This bold move requires the commitment of staff and resources. Organizing your activities to align with the step-by-step process outlined in this book will help ensure visible progress. The next chapter outlines some of the more typical "wake-up calls" to usability that companies experience. An exploration of some of the more common reactions to these experiences is valuable for capitalizing on initial momentum.

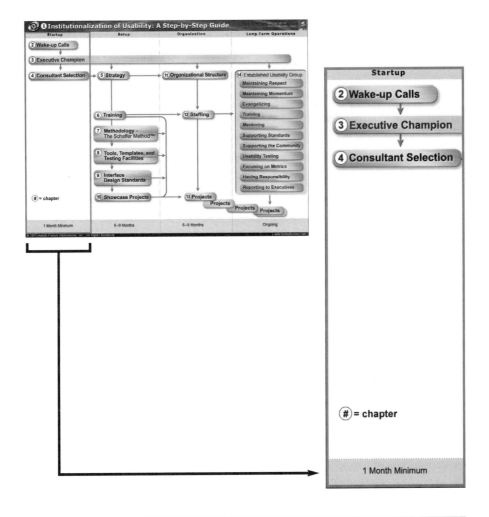

Startup

2 **Wake-up Calls**

3 **Executive Champion**

4 **Consultant Selection**

(#) = chapter

1 Month Minimum

Part I

Startup

The Startup phase is about bringing attention to the issue of usability and aligning the mandatory executive and consultant resources to start a usability initiative.

The institutionalization of usability starts with a wake-up call. Be it reading a book or experiencing a disaster, the attention of the organization needs to move toward the issue of usability.

Among those experienced in the field of usability, there seems to be total agreement about the criticality of an executive champion. This champion should not be a lone evangelist in the trenches—the champion should be someone high enough in the executive suite to have a real impact on the corporate focus and the ability to bring a strategic level of resources to bear on the problem. Without this executive, there is little hope of meaningful long-term success.

The executive champion provides direction, resources, focus, and accountability. However, the executive also needs an operational team that has expertise and resources in the field of usability. While it might be possible to recruit usability staff and build an infrastructure from scratch, it is often better to start with an experienced usability professional to guide you. This professional should have access to an experienced and integrated team and a full set of methods, tools, templates, and standards to help you build your infrastructure.

Chapter 2

Wake-up Calls and Common Reactions

- ➤ There is no question that user-centered design is worthwhile.

- ➤ There are a number of ways to get your organization moving toward the institutionalization of usability. Try to pick one of the less painful and less expensive wake-up calls.

- ➤ The different types of wake-up calls include train wrecks, executive insights, new staff, education and training, expert reviews, usability testing, and new technologies.

- ➤ Wake-up calls leave people wanting to move forward. Don't fall for usability fads or half measures.

The fact that you are reading this book suggests you probably know that there is an iron-clad case for usability engineering. However, I will review the arguments for the value and criticality of this work so you will have this information readily available when you need to convince others that usability is worthwhile. But keep in mind that it is very rare to find an organization that decides to do serious usability work based solely on numeric calculations (like ROI). Most organizations seem to need more—they need a real breakthrough.

Some organizations need a disaster before they can get serious about usability. Your organization may have already experienced a wake-up call, or perhaps you recognize your company needs to do something about usability. This chapter describes the logical argument for usability and then describes some of the ways companies first get their attention drawn to usability. The chapter also outlines a set of special pitfalls that typically surface when companies decide to seriously address usability but then go for a quick fix.

The wake-up call is not complete until there is an executive champion who arises to manage the overall institutionalization of usability.

The Value of Usability

The need for usability is very real. In general, both consumers and technology companies have accepted that if a product is easy to use, it sells more and requires less maintenance. There was a time when you often needed to argue that point. Not any more. Usability specialists ensure that software is practical and useful. But primarily, usability work focuses on user experience and performance. These elements can be measured and quantified in terms of the user's:

- Speed
- Accuracy
- Training requirements (or self-evidency)
- Satisfaction
- Safety

By applying usability engineering methods, you can build a site or an application that is practical, useful, usable, and satisfying.

In a *Dilbert* comic strip, Scott Adams had Dilbert present his manager with a tough choice: Either spend a million dollars to fix the incomprehensible interface, or close your eyes and wish real hard the users won't care. The manager is left with eyes closed, wishing intensely, and thereby saving all that money.

Usability does require an investment. It costs money to provide staff, training, standards, tools, and a user-centered process. It takes time to establish the infrastructure. You may need to hire consultants and new staff.

Is it worth spending this money and time setting up a usability effort? It is common for a usable Web site to sell 100% or more than an unusable one [Nielsen and Gilutz 2003]. It is typical to find site traffic, productivity, and function usage more than double. Unfortunately, it is also common to see developers build applications that users then reject because of lack of usability. For example, among HFI's clients, we recently have seen a new sign-up process for a major service provider that had a 97% drop-off rate and a voice response system at a bank that had only a 3% usage level. There is no question that usability work is insurance against these types of multimillion-dollar disasters.

If you follow a user-centered design process, you can expect to spend about 10% of the overall project budget on usability work [Nielsen and Gilutz 2003]. This includes everything—from evaluation of previous and competitive designs to data gathering with users to the design of the structure, standards, and detailed screens. It also includes usability testing.

There is a lot of work to do, and 10% is a big fraction of the budget. But the good news is that the overall money and time required to create an acceptable site or application is unlikely to increase. In fact, the cost is likely to go down for several reasons, including those discussed in the following subsections.

Reducing Design Cycles

Today, it is still common to have projects that require major rework because the application does not meet user needs or is unintelligible to users. Implementing good usability practices greatly reduces the chances of having to rework the design. The cost of retrofitting a user interface is always staggering. The cost can be substantial if the detailed design must be improved. But these changes in wording, layout, control selection, color, and graphics are minor compared with the creation of a new interface structure.

When people use a Web site, Web application, software, camera, or remote control, the part of the product that the human interacts with is the **interface**. The interface, therefore, is the part of the product that gets the most usability attention. The **interface structure** determines the interface design—it defines the paths and navigation that the user of the product will take to find information or perform a task. If usability engineering is not applied at the start of interface design, the interface structure is where serious usability problems emerge. Since 80% of the usability of an interface is a function of its structure,[1] a retrofit often amounts to a redevelopment of the entire presentation layer. That is why the best solution is to design the interface right the first time.

Avoiding Building Unnecessary Functions

Often, users evaluate software by a checklist of features, and companies feel compelled to include these features to be competitive. However, companies often find that users do not need or want certain functions. Discovering this earlier—*before* the product is fully designed or coded—makes the user interface better because there are fewer functions to manage, and the interface can become cleaner. There is also a huge savings in development and maintenance costs. The unnecessary functions need not be designed, coded, tested, and maintained.

Expediting Decision Making

There is a great deal of research that indicates how best to design interfaces. For example, it is well known that using all capital letters slows reading speed by 14–20% [Tinker 1965, 1963], that using three nouns in a row confuses people [Waite 1982], and that users expect

---

1. This data is based on HFI's 20 years of experience in the field of usability, across thousands of consulting projects.

to find the home button at the top left corner of Web pages [Bernard 2002]. This means the development team need not spend hours second-guessing these kinds of design decisions. Being familiar with these and other usability research principles saves development and testing time and helps contribute to a more usable product.

Increasing Sales

If you are developing a product for sale, a usable product will sell more. If you are developing a Web site to sell a product or service, a usable Web site will sell more product and services. Usable products mean more sales. For example, an insurance company has a Web site that is currently feeding 10 leads a day to the insurance agents. The company could feed 15 leads a day, but the site has some usability problems, and the company is losing 5 leads a day. This is due to visitors dropping out because they can't figure out how to contact an agent or finish using the "insurance quoting application" on the site. If usability is routine in the organization and those usability problems are fixed and/or prevented, how much would the company be able to increase sales? The answer can be determined through a few simple calculations.

1. The company estimates it is losing at least 5 leads a day from usability problems, which is 1,825 leads a year.
2. The company assumes that for every 5 leads received, it can get 1 customer. This means the company is losing 365 customers a year.
3. Each customer provides an average of $600 in income from premiums per year. This means the company could increase sales in the first year by $219,000.
4. Using an average customer retention time of 12 years, fixing the current usability problems could increase the company's sales during those 12 years by $2,628,000.

Avoiding "Reinventing the Wheel"

Good usability engineering, much like all other engineering processes, means designing with reusable templates. There is no need to reinvent the conventions for the design of menus, forms, wizards, and so on. This saves design time. Also, because it is easy to create reusable code around these templates, they save development and testing time as well.

Avoiding Disasters

Users are highly adaptable. Even when an interface is poorly designed, some users have enough motivation to keep trying to use the product. Sometimes they manage to use remarkably complex and awkward applications. But sometimes a design is completely rejected. The people who are supposed to use the product may refuse to stick with it; instead they go back to their old ways of getting the task done, buy elsewhere, or just give up. These are usability and product disasters. It's best to get it right the first time.

For all these reasons, the 10% of the budget that you should be spending on usability work is easily saved on every project, in addition to the improved value of the end design. Even if you take into account only the typical savings from working with reusable templates, usability work pays for itself—it is really *free*. However, the decision to begin institutionalizing usability requires more than a simple calculation of the benefits involved. The organization—and particularly the executives in the organization—need a deeper understanding of how implementing usability means changing the way business is done. For this realization to occur, a strong wake-up call is often required.

Usability within the Medical Industry

By Dr. Ed Israelski, Program Manager—
Human Factors, Abbott Laboratories

Usability or "human factors" are important to Abbott in two ways. One, the competitive landscape is such that more and more of our main competitors are putting an emphasis on their safe products that they are also easy to use and learn. The second way involves the FDA and the safety regulations that

Abbott must follow. If it were just the regulations, people could find loopholes; but combine the regulatory requirements with the business case supporting human factors, and it's a good one-two punch.

Also, there are standards, such as the medical device standards, out there. An important organization called AAMI (the Association for the Advancement of Medical Instrumentation, www.aami.org) develops standards and training courses for the medical device industry. One of the standards it has developed is a human factors standard. This process standard, which came out last year, is called "ANSI/AAMI HE 74:2001 Human factors design process for medical devices." Now I can refer to the standard's human factors step and build it into the budget and product development schedule because it's a standard and the FDA will be looking for it. Then we can also show that it makes good business sense as well. We can show financial benefits because it saves money on training, produces fewer recalls, reduces liability exposure, and increases customers' satisfaction so they come back to buy more—all of which are important things.

If you institutionalize usability, you give people tools and methods and resources, including internal and external personnel. Then it's easy for people to do this—it's the path of least resistance. They don't feel they have to question it and make a business case each time they decide to put human factors process steps in the development project. So, if you institutionalize it, the decision-making process becomes more efficient.

Types of Wake-up Calls

My favorite part about teaching usability courses is that magic moment when course participants "get it." I can see it in their eyes: the usability paradigm clicks in and suddenly their whole perspective changes. They return from breaks and comment on design issues such as confusing elevator controls and bathroom fixtures, and I know they will never be quite the same. It is the same thing with organizations. There is a point where the organization gets it—the organization wakes up and sees the user-centered perspective as essential, and that organization will never be the same.

In most organizations, the wake-up call cannot be instantaneous because there are too many people involved. But when the wake-up call does happen, it draws the attention of the organization to the important issues. There is realization, excitement, and determination. Resources are allocated and people start working on an entire institutionalization effort, or at least on addressing some of the major usability concerns. So while a wake-up call might cause some discomfort, it's often the first step required to institutionalize usability. The subsections below describe different types of wake-up calls that organizations may experience.

Train Wrecks

Train wrecks are the most expensive type of wake-up call: The feature-rich product that looked great in concept proves to be impractical and unusable, but this discovery comes too late. This is the most dramatic kind of wake-up call, and if left unaddressed, it can create serious or even catastrophic events. These problems can be embarrassing, expensive, brand destroying, potentially dangerous for users, and may even cause the collapse of your company [Casey 1993].

At the beginning of 2000, there was a frightening downturn in the high technology field. This was bound to happen. The industry had created thousands of feature-rich products that turned out to be impractical and unusable applications and Web sites. Users found it more difficult and frustrating to buy groceries online than to go out to the supermarket. It was still easier to use a paper calendar than a PDA. The wireless revolution slowed because users didn't like taking minutes to click through a long list of menus just to get a stock quote. The sad news is that many of these companies never had the opportunity to get a wake-up call: Even before the usability doctor could be called, they were ready for the mortician.

If your company hasn't suffered from a train wreck (and I certainly hope it hasn't), it is important that your company prevent a disaster by choosing to implement one of the other types of wake-up calls described in the following subsections.

Executive Insights

Executives are in an interesting position. Typically, they are not directly involved in the design process, so their fresh perspective often allows them to notice that a given design will make no sense to customers. In contrast, sometimes the staff members involved in detailed design become so wrapped up in the design that they veer away from customers' or users' needs and become distracted by other issues such as technical constraints, time deadlines, or just certain ways of thinking. Executives are usually not involved in as detailed a way, and therefore they can catch issues more easily.

However, executives can also have an unproductive reaction and become angry and disparaging toward the developers. Some executives also have a tendency to believe that the right answer is to step in and design the product personally. But some executives have read a good article on usability or received respected advice from a friend. They realize that there is a profession of usability engineers, and this insight starts them on a productive path. With sound knowledge of the field in hand, an executive can institute a wake-up call that will prove to be priceless for the corporation or agency. He or she can be the one to say, "Wait, there are some critical issues we have missed. We haven't paid enough attention to the human component. We need to make this and all of our technology really easy to use." The executive thereby institutes the wake-up call that allows the organization to begin incorporating a more user-centered approach.

New Staff

Another type of wake-up call that is less disruptive and painful than a train wreck is cross-pollination from new hires. For example, Armando Ortiz is an executive specializing in IT strategy. He first hired a usability vendor while working at Discover Financial

Services (Discover Card). He then moved to McDonald's, and then BP AMOCO. At each new position, he immediately became an evangelist for usability and consistency in design. He was able to share the previous company's wake-up call and was able to point to past successes.

There is a significant advantage to hiring new staff with practical experience of institutionalization programs in other companies. It can save you the major expense of needing a train wreck or disastrous project to get the organization's attention. This alone can be worth millions of dollars.

Education and Training

In the process of institutionalization, you need to use training to internalize skills and knowledge. Usability engineering starts with a mindset, but this mindset is not the only element involved. Usability calls upon a body of knowledge, and designers and developers need a particular knowledge and skill set in order to quickly and effectively apply usability principles to their designs.

There is also another value to training—it can serve as a wake-up call. A management briefing on the critical issues in usability, for example, may provide a vicarious wake-up call. Or perhaps a class taken by a developer may discuss the benefits of usability testing. Any of these encounters with usability can shine a light on the intersection between technology and people and thereby also highlight the fact that the organization needs to take action.

Expert Reviews

Expert reviews, usually completed by a consultant, succeed very well as relatively painless wake-up calls. It is useful to have reviews performed by outsiders—it makes the review less personal and less influenced by politics, and it is less possible to hold a grudge against an external source.

In an expert review, a consultant systematically evaluates an application or Web site based on established usability engineering models,

Experiencing the Wake-up Call and Beginning a Usability Process

By Pat Malecek, AVP, CUA, User Experience Manager,
A.G. Edwards & Sons, Inc.

In 1999 we began a process to greatly and ambitiously reengineer our public and client-facing Web presence. An army of us just plunged right in and started marching right along. In the eleventh hour, we solicited an expert review from an external source. That expert review said that one of the critical applications, or critical pieces of our new Web presence, was unusable. And by the way, you need some usability people.

If I look back, I'm pretty sure that was the impetus for the creation of what has become my team and a recognition of usability issues. Almost immediately thereafter—within months—we had brought in training and crystallized the efforts.

I remember reading Eric's white paper, "The Institutionalization of Usability" [Schaffer 2001], and thinking, this really sets the course for what we're up against. That paper says that going through the institutionalization process takes about two years. From the hard lessons I mentioned before up to today, it has been about two years.

What steps have we taken? Well, we obviously hired people who had the skills or at least closely matched the skills we needed. Then we brought in multiple training opportunities to our campus. We've also sent people out for training. We have endeavored to incorporate my team and usability practices into the development methodology. We have representation on various committees that steer development, and we're also represented on essentially all Web-based projects. Our usability team is located within the Internet Services Department (ISD). ISD basically owns the Internet channel—anything that's delivered via the Internet or our intranet. We are involved as much as possible in everything that channel delivers.

principles, and research. The review tends to show a whole new way of seeing the application. The user-centered approach has a different perspective and a different technology, and is a valuable way to direct short-term improvements to an application or site. Expert reviews are most valuable in providing an inexpensive and fairly painless wake-up call.

Usability Testing

Usability testing may be the first time a company actually sees new users use the products. While this testing has the potential to be embarrassing or upsetting, it can also provide an effective wake-up call.

For example, Figure 2-1 illustrates the results of a usability test of the Web site of a major auto manufacturer.[2] The results were very obvious: Users were unable to complete what should have been straightforward and simple tasks.

New Technologies

Attention to usability can be a side benefit of various new initiatives. Obtaining a new technology can force an organization to focus on usability and create an opportunity to fix poorly designed interfaces. For example, higher screen resolution can raise the issue of how to take advantage of the increased capability and lead to a round of improved designs. A new voice recognition system can easily raise questions of proper ergonomic design. These events move the company toward attention to usability.

A whole set of special concerns can also drive attention to usability. For example, interest in accessibility for the visually impaired and the legislation requiring support of Web site readers can create side questions. Once attention is drawn to a usability issue, there is a good chance that the whole value of user-centered design will show up on the corporate radar.

---

2. Data taken from an HFI usability test of a major auto manufacturer's Web site, completed in 2002.

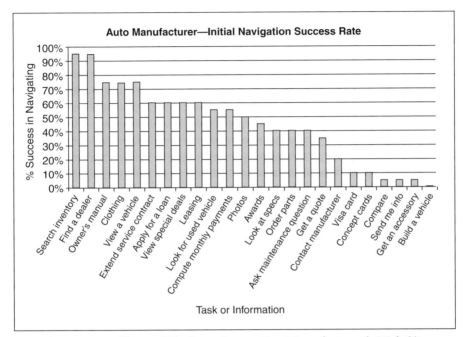

Figure 2-1: *Chart of Findings from a Car Manufacturer's Web Site. Only One-Third of the Users Could Get a Quote.*

Common Responses to Wake-up Calls

Once you get the wake-up call, you will be moved to another track. Your organization will bring its attention to the issue of usability and will want to move ahead quickly. You will hear many ideas for usability enhancement, but many will be ineffective or at best provide an incomplete solution.

Companies often try to achieve usability with fads, hoping that the latest technology will make software usable. When color monitors became available, some people suggested that color coding would make everything clear. These "designs" cluttered screens with so many colors that they degraded user performance. Others suggested that usability would be solved if the background were blue.

Computer-based training (CBT) was initially seen as a solution to the problem of usability. People thought that it was even possible to train users to use confusing software interfaces.

When graphical user interfaces (GUIs) first appeared, around 1984, many people felt that the availability of windows, icons, mice, and pointing devices would make all interfaces user friendly.

Some professionals initially thought that the Web would provide a simple set of conventions known by all users that would make usable design easy. In reality, the Web so far has amazingly diverse designs, poorly established conventions, and millions of sites that aren't usable.

Most people learn by hard experience that there are no simple technical solutions. In fact, there are no simple solutions at all; there is no magic pill to make software usable. Once companies realize that there is no magic solution that ensures usability, they begin to try more reasonable approaches.

Unfortunately, even some of the more reasonable approaches are not fully successful. Below are some of the common pitfalls into which organizations fall. You will want to avoid these.

Relying on Good Intentions

Many managers start with this approach because it is attractive, not to mention cheap. It seems logical to think you can tell staff members to "put the customer first" or "be customer centric" and then expect them to just be able to do it. The problem is that they can't just do it.

Creating usable designs takes far more than good intentions. Today, virtually everyone in the development field wants good usability, but usability is hard to achieve. The proof is the awful designs that are so commonplace. Highly motivated professionals often inadvertently create usability disasters.

Just motivating people won't result in usability. In some cases a manager taking this path needs to see a whole project built under his or

---

Being an Advocate for the Process

By Dana Griffith, CUA, Web Consultant—Interactive Media,
American Electric Power

One of the principles I have gained from usability training is that you should never become the advocate for the user. I thought that was really interesting because at the time I was sitting there during the session thinking, of course I'm supposed to be the advocate for the user. But the idea presented was that, once you become the advocate for the user, people try to go around you. They just really don't want to stop what they are doing and change things. But if you simply become an advocate for the *technology* or the *process* and let people decide what they're going to do with that, you will have better success.

Becoming an advocate for the process can have very practical applications. Perhaps we're looking at a very simple application on a Web site (a form, for example), and someone wants to know whether one area should be populated already or whether it should drop down with selections. In this type of scenario, I can say to the people involved in that project, "I can test that for you tomorrow and find out."

---

her well-intentioned motivation, only to find that usability has not been greatly improved. In other cases, the manager reviewing the designs can immediately see that the designs are unintelligible. It takes a serious application of usability engineering technology and methods to ensure that an organization's program will be successful.

Relying on Testing

Sometimes companies get the idea that all they need is usability testing. It is good to be able to test, but testing alone is not enough. Testing pinpoints problems in the design and its usability that can be fixed. But to be successful and to institutionalize usability, companies need a complete methodology including concept development, data gathering, structural design, design standards, and so on. While usability testing is important, by itself it's not a long-term solution.

Relying on Training

It makes sense. You have smart people who know the domain and technology, so you think you can just give them some training in usability, and things will be fine. If you pick a good program, training will help, and the staff will learn a good set of basic skills.

The key word here is *basic*. You will probably give people three to ten days of training. In this time frame, they are not about to become doctors of user interface design. They will instead be paramedics. The trained staff members will see the problems clearly. As a result, they will create better designs, but they will still feel frustrated. The corporate culture won't have changed enough to value usability, and there will be no plan for usability in the corporate system development life cycle. There will be no design standards. Organizational channels won't be provided for testing with users. There will be no one to call with questions and no repository of examples and templates. The staff members will know when something isn't quite right, but they probably won't know how to fix it.

Relying on Repair Jobs

Repair jobs try to fix usability problems at the last minute. This is inefficient and creates only limited potential for improvement. Ideally, usability work starts when the requirements are defined. If you bring usability engineering into the process late, you can improve small pieces of the design like the wording, layout, color, graphics, and control selection. Unfortunately, there will be no time for more profound changes like standardizing user interface elements, the flow of logic, or other major elements.

Relying on Projects by Ad Agencies

Another common response to addressing usability concerns is to bring in the advertising agency with which the organization already works. But ad agencies currently have few real usability specialists. The ad agency will be able to help with branding and perception issues, but advertising is a different skill set than usability work. There is some overlap in that both advertising and usability staff members are focused on the customer, but the goals of the ad agency and the goals of the usability team are not always identical. The methods and processes that each group uses to complete its work are very different. Bringing in an ad agency will not spread usability throughout the organization and may not delve deep enough into navigation structures to even improve task usability on a single project. Usability focuses on whether users can perform certain tasks with the technology product. Advertising concentrates on capturing and focusing attention, communicating brand, and influencing behavior. Advertising and usability efforts should work hand in hand, but they are not the same.

Hiring Usability Consultants

A common response after a wake-up call is hiring a consultant to review a Web site or application. This might be a good starting point and will probably help with a particular project, but it won't address the problems of the next application or Web site. Bringing in a consultant on one project is not going to disseminate usability engineering throughout the organization.

These consultants can be expected to do a good job and can be cost-effective. However, hiring consultants still leaves the client company without internal capabilities. The company may see the value of the good design work, but it will have to call back the usability team for each new project.

Some usability consultants try to transfer knowledge to the client organization. Following this practice does help company staff see that good usability practice does make a difference. But realistically, without training, standards, and tools, this approach leaves little behind that is enduringly useful.

Hiring New Usability Staff

With a clear understanding of the competitive value of usability work, managers sometimes make the substantial commitment of hiring usability staff. This is laudable but, unfortunately, it often fails. The manager may not be able to find or screen for experienced usability specialists. Some people looking for work in usability believe that experience with one project that involved usability means they are qualified to be a usability specialist. Yet becoming an effective usability practitioner takes an educational foundation (e.g., cognitive psychology), specific training in usability work (e.g., expert review, structural design), and a period of mentoring by a seasoned expert. After attaining a master's degree in the field, it generally takes three to five years of mentored experience before totally independent work is advisable.

It is all too easy to hire people who need a lot more experience, training, and mentoring before they will be effective. Hiring one such staff member is time consuming enough. You don't want to end up with an entire usability group that is immature or inexperienced.

Typically, a manager hires one or two people to start. Even if the new hires are experienced, having only one or two people often means that the "group" is quickly besieged and rendered ineffective. The team members may soon be so busy that they can't get design standards in place and may not have resources to provide training.

In situations like this, it is best to have many of the initial activities completed by outside consultants who have an established team that has specialized skills in training and standards development and can work quickly and successfully. The consultants will be seen as outsiders, and employees may be more willing to have an outsider dissect the flaws in their designs. Outsiders can say things that an insider has left unsaid. The consultants will be there to get the internal usability staff going on the right path and can hand over their expertise and knowledge to help the internal staff become established.

If you install a usability team, your efforts should include more than just hiring the people to staff it. Making the team members effective means positioning them to be an integral and harmonious part of the organization, establishing clear roles and authority, and addressing the integration of this team with the other parts of the workforce.

Seeing the Real Numbers Creates a Call to Action Too

By Harley Manning, Research Director, Forrester Research

Let's say you do care about usability—the organizations we surveyed don't have a formal process for evaluating the usability of the packaged applications when they come in. They're not looking at the cost of ownership with regards to usability, typically—and even if they do care about it, they don't know how to evaluate it.

So, knowing that in theory it costs me money to have poor usability and being able to actually evaluate how poor the usability is and put a number on it, that's the huge gap. Once you do that and start looking at what the real numbers are, then you say, "I must do something about this!" But that's what the organizations we surveyed haven't done yet.

Usability is clearly worthwhile. But how will your organization reach this deep understanding and become willing to act? People in some organizations may actively seek out usability as a powerful innovation. They may read an article or book and be on their way to full institutionalization. Others may begin to employ user-centered activities as the result of a disastrous experience. Regardless of the background, it is important to be conscious of your organization's reaction to the initial call to usability to make sure that you avoid some of the more common pitfalls. The next chapter explores the necessity of identifying an executive champion in order to secure the success of your ongoing efforts.

Chapter 3

The Executive Champion

> Find an executive champion who will move the usability effort forward. The champion must:
>
> ▷ Get trained in the basics of usability
>
> ▷ Understand and evangelize the specific value of usability to the organization
>
> ▷ Understand the current development process and how usability will fit in
>
> ▷ Expect and acknowledge resistance to the institutionalization process
>
> ▷ Keep the initiative moving long term
>
> The champion may transition to a full Chief User Experience Officer (CXO) role, with responsibility and control over all aspects of the customer's engagement with your organization.

In any corporate change there needs to be a leader who provides direction, support, and political management—this is the executive champion. The executive champion has to be an executive high enough in the organization to move the resources and culture forward. If you are in the position to be the executive champion, this chapter will help you understand the task ahead of you. If you are an individual contributor who cares about usability and wants to move the effort forward, getting executive sponsorship should be at the top of your agenda.

The Role of the Executive Champion

The executive champion might be the most challenging role in the entire institutionalization effort. There will probably be no formal position and authority, and the organization may not have even begun the process of sensitization and assimilation. Yet the executive champion must gather resources, create a strategy, and keep the process moving. He or she has to manage points of contention and chart the course to full acceptance.

Without a champion, the usability staff often has a hard time being included as part of a cohesive strategic effort. The presence of a good executive champion is the best predictor of the success of a usability institutionalization effort because, without a usability champion, the usability group does not have access to key players in the organization. To be successful, the usability group has to effect change within the organization; without a champion at the executive level, this achievement is nearly impossible. With an executive champion, the group has a chance to create change and obtain the visibility needed to succeed.

The executive champion doesn't need a background in usability engineering or software development, but he or she does need to understand the value of usability, its proper applications, and the importance of an implementation strategy. It is possible to get a sufficient foundation in usability engineering from a short course and some reading. The champion must first and foremost have a clear understanding of the business imperatives of the organization and must see how usability work supports these objectives. He or she should understand the core value of usability in the organization and repeatedly reinforce this focus, with examples showing how usability will reduce call time or increase sales.

The champion keeps the whole effort focused on the business goal. I have often found that this is the differentiator between an effective executive champion and an ineffective one. Ineffective champions say, "We need usability." This is nice, but the reality is that *no business ever needs usability*. Effective executive champions say, "We need to sell more, get fewer returns, and reduce support costs." They know the specific things their business needs. They say this over and over, thousands of times. The business focus of the usability effort is their mantra—and it works.

The executive champion needs to be able to effectively influence the key people in the organization's power structure. This means arranging for project funding as well as convincing key people in an organization whose approval and support are necessary for the institutionalization program to succeed. The executive champion needs to employ approaches that work best with each person— understanding individuals' hot buttons and learning styles.

The executive champion must guide the usability staff through the project approval and selling process. The champion needs to check for acceptance and detect areas of resistance at all levels of the organization. The executive champion is the key agent of change and therefore must be able to network with key people in the company, detect areas of resistance before resistance occurs, remove organizational obstacles as they arise, and work continuously to promote acceptance. These skills are essential.

The executive champion must be responsible for the institutionalization strategy. This means identifying the staging of usability work and ensuring the allocation of responsibilities and resources. A good strategy is critically important (see Chapter 5), but beyond the content of the strategy, the champion must monitor progress and demand results. Progress happens when an executive regularly asks for updates and checks milestones, keeping the staff members on task. The executive champion cannot create a strategy and forget it. He or she must firmly ensure that the team carries out the strategy.

Why Support from Senior Management Is Crucial

By Harley Manning, Research Director, Forrester Research

The person at the top of the organization must believe that user experience is important and must require people to follow good practices. Unless that person is committed to this idea, good usability is not going to happen.

The companies that really get it tend to have C-level[1] people who care deeply, like Charles Schwab. Charles Schwab himself, the guy who runs the company, uses the site every day. The woman who headed up the site design came to a workshop I ran a few years ago. She said that Schwab called down on a pretty much daily basis. Certainly, she didn't go a week without hearing directly from him about some problem that he or his mother or his friend had with the site or about something he thought could be better. So this guy is very engaged, very demanding. And the site works as well as it does because, from the top down, it's critically important that the site deliver a great user experience.

We come back to this time and again—the executives must understand the importance of user experience to the business. Because no executives will put up their hands and say, let's do something that's bad for business, or let's do something that hurts our customers—they won't do that on purpose. When they do those things, they do them out of ignorance.

You don't get widespread attention to user experience unless its importance is understood at the top. That's where the leverage is.

---

1. "C-level" refers to executive-level staff or those who bear the name "Chief" within their titles. Examples include CEO, CFO, and CMO.

Deciding to Innovate

To be successful, key executives cannot just avert problems and maintain the operation. They must find new methods, create new ways of working, and make new markets and business models. Without innovation, they are caretakers, not executives.

Executives identify areas of innovation in many ways. They react based on their experience, read industry journals, attend conferences, and talk to colleagues and friends. Executives are thereby exposed to thousands of ideas, yet they can respond to only a tiny fraction of these with direct action. There are enough resources to cover only a few major changes each year. The executive's job is to select ideas that will really make a difference to the company. Selecting usability as the idea to move forward with can have a large impact.

Creating usable software can be a huge market differentiator, or it may be the only way to keep up with the competition. Usability can save millions of dollars when there are large numbers of internal users. For example, the usability team at SUN Microsystems estimated that poor design of the company intranet cost the average employee 6 minutes a day, for a total of $10 million in lost time per year [Ward 2001]. A single second removed from the average call-handling time can be worth $50,000 a year or more in large call centers.[2] With an application that has a large number of users, small improvements can add up fast. It is no accident that *usability* has become a common term discussed in executive suites. Once the executive champion determines the specific value of usability to the organization, he or she must spread the word and keep people focused on the goal.

---

2. "The bane of such IVR (Interactive Voice Response) systems occurs when the caller presses the '0' button. Because when the customer service representative (CSR) speaks with the caller, they start the 'cost-meter.' Each second carries a significant loaded labor rate. Some of our corporate customers have indicated that every second they save on the average length of a call means a saving[s] of $120,000 a year. Where CSR employees number in the thousands, savings per second have been reported at a million dollars a year! (Yes, we were surprised, too.)" [Schaffer et al. 1999]

Making the Change

There is no way to institutionalize usability without making waves. The design of user interfaces is likely to be an emotional issue for a number of people because they have serious time and ego investments in the way design has been done in the past. In many organizations, user interface design has occurred by a political process that has little to do with user needs but requires a lot of effort put into negotiation and power balancing. The group members who created this delicate compromise will probably resist change.

As the application development community moves towards a systematic usability engineering process, there will be resistance. People will fear that their work isn't valued, and they may exhibit defensive behavior. It is important to let these feelings surface and to confront them directly. To reduce resistance, introduce usability practices as new technology and present them like any other new initiative.

Another useful approach is having an external consultant in the mix; some employees find it easier to accept criticism and new methods from an outsider than from peers. Staff members should be applauded for their ability to incorporate the new insights into their process, and those who show commitment can become part of the core of the ongoing effort.

Some suggestions for making the change include the following.

- Anticipate the points of resistance so they will not surprise you when they occur.
- Make sure the executive champion understands these points of resistance ahead of time so he or she can be ready to move when necessary.
- Involve key players in other parts of the organization early. If the person in charge of programmers, for instance, participates in the usability planning, that removes one area of resistance from the start.
- Be willing to change as the group matures. What works at the beginning of the process as the group is new and renegade may

need to be adjusted later. Some of the activities that the group members do themselves initially, for example, may eventually need to be outsourced or turned over to others.

- Think of usability as an evolution. You may not be able to get it all immediately. Plan for the stages of growth and acceptance rather than insisting that everyone in the organization follow usability principles and processes immediately.

- Work within your normal organizational change process. How does change happen successfully in your organization? To introduce usability, follow the same processes you used the last time you successfully implemented a new idea.

Educating the Executives

Even though the executive champion needs to be the executive who is most familiar with usability, the champion's message is most easily heard and heeded if other key executives in the organization understand what usability is trying to accomplish. Few CEOs or senior executives are usability engineers by training or profession. Therefore, almost all executives must learn about the value of usability. This means understanding, very concretely, how usability insights impact company performance and position.

This process does not have to take a long time, but exposure to real-life examples is essential. Executives need to be able to interpret user-oriented metrics and understand that usability is neither easy nor just a matter of common sense. Executives must care about usability and see usability as a key business objective. Executive-level briefings and short courses designed specifically for management are helpful, as are periodic meetings with key executives to share the results of the first showcase projects and ongoing programs. The briefings should provide general concepts and examples from other organizations. It is also important to include more specific, concrete examples—presenting real cases from your organization, for example, is compelling.

The executive champion as well as other executives in the organization have specific training needs. The executive champion should receive more training than other executives and should also complete some further reading. In addition to the management briefing that all the executives should receive, it is worthwhile for the executive champion to get some formal training in usability engineering. The executive champion can also sit in on a few days of a course for practitioners. Reading about the field is also of great benefit for all executives.

Several books provide excellent background reading about usability engineering. A few of these selected readings are valuable for either the executive or the executive champion. These titles, followed by a brief description, are listed below.

Valuable books for all executives:

- *The Inmates Are Running the Asylum: Why High-Tech Products Drive Us Crazy and How to Restore the Sanity,* by Alan Cooper [1999]. A book for executives and project managers about why usability matters. Written by "the Father of Visual Basic."

- *The Design of Everyday Things,* by Donald Norman [1988]. A broad look at how human factors affects the design of everything we come into contact with.

- *Set Phasers on Stun: And Other True Tales of Design, Technology, and Human Error,* by Steven Casey [1993]. A compelling compilation of 20 true stories that explore the ramifications of interface design decisions.

Valuable books for executive champions:

- *Don't Make Me Think: A Common Sense Approach to Web Usability,* by Steve Krug [2000]. A short, powerful book appropriate for the executive champion on the basics of what makes Web sites usable.

- *Usability Engineering,* by Jakob Nielsen [1994]. A basic primer on usability engineering, with some early metrics.

- *Homepage Usability: 50 Websites Deconstructed,* by Jakob Nielsen and Marie Tahir [2001]. A visual look at some of the most popular public Web sites.

- *Cost-Justifying Usability*, by Randolph Bias and Deborah Mayhew [1994]. Different ideas on how to calculate the cost benefits of usability work.

Keeping It Moving Long Term

There is an ongoing need for leadership. Resistance to the usability effort often won't appear until the infrastructure is in place and people have to start changing their design conventions, methods, and development schedules.

It is easy for usability programs to lose steam. Usability committees may spend so much time and effort creating a standards document that they don't have the energy to disseminate and support it. Usability groups may get discouraged by fighting turf battles or having to say the same things over and over. Building a successful usability program requires ongoing commitment.

As the effort matures, expectations will change. In the early days, specific wins and before/after comparisons will be proof of success. For example, an organization's previously labeled "problem" application may now be loudly appreciated by the customers or in-house users. As time goes on, business-related metrics, ROI calculations, and results of user satisfaction surveys and sales data will become measures of success.

Getting Middle Management on Board with Usability

By Janice Nall, Chief, Communication Technologies Branch, National Cancer Institute

We've got a usability engineering department here at the National Cancer Institute, and there is support from on high. People like our director are saying the right words and being supportive of it. The next step is to translate that message down to middle management to get resources, tools, and the ability to move forward. We need to make it more than lip service and to

(continued)

Getting Middle Management on Board with Usability (cont.)

make it so integrated into the development cycle for communication products that, just as you would not consider putting up a Web site without having somebody "QC"[3] it or run multiple platform testing, you would not let a site go live without designing it through usability engineering.

The Office of Communications has been in a huge transition. The previous director didn't know anything about usability but was sold on the concept immediately after hearing about it. We actually arranged for her to be in the room during testing and to watch videos. Even though she wasn't a technical person, we got her support. Plus, we have taken a business approach. Usability saves money: We can show how usability saves clicks, we can show how it saves time, and we can show how it saves development money.

Who's going to say that they're against something that will make our cancer information more usable for all audiences? Nobody is going to be against it, but we need to help people in middle management understand what every agency needs to accomplish that. We need qualified staff and qualified contractors, and we need a portable lab, a permanent lab, or access to a lab we can rent. When we can get 40 people in a room from 40 different offices across the National Institutes of Health, as we do with our training and education sessions, we immediately sow the seeds of this concept, and the participants are always hungry for more. Then they can start working on their management. We try to do it kind of "grassroots up," and we have the support of senior management. However, it's that middle layer that's hard to get into meetings, hard to convince to see the testing, hard to communicate this message to. It's not the Web community, and it's not even the communications community—it really is the middle layer of management.

---

3. "QC" refers to quality control.

Becoming a CXO

The payoff for being the executive champion may come in the form of a promotion to the role of CXO. This is a new role that is just being discussed by forward-thinking companies. It is unique in that a CXO can move with authority throughout all divisions of the organization in the quest for an optimal customer experience. The CXO can go to each line of business and drive it to follow standards and push for consistency between print media, Web, and store layouts. The CXO is responsible for the customer experience and has authority to make the changes needed. In addition, the CXO manages the central usability team and perhaps other teams, like graphics, that are needed to reach the goal of presenting a coherent face to the customer.

Obtaining executive sponsorship is a crucial element in moving the institutionalization process forward. By establishing the role of executive champion (and later, the role of CXO), your organization not only demonstrates commitment to a user-centered design process but also ensures that some of the more common areas of resistance will be addressed. The next chapter provides guidance on what to look for when choosing an outside consultant to jump-start your efforts with valuable expertise.

Chapter 4

Selecting a Usability Consultant

➤ Outside consultants are important to usability institutionalization—they can do things no insider can do.

➤ Retain a usability consultancy early in the process to provide infrastructure and jump-start the institutionalization process.

➤ There are many usability consultancies, and there are huge differences in capability, resources, and fit with your culture. Pick the right consultancy for your organization.

➤ A good consultant guides your strategy, sets up your infrastructure, helps develop your staff and internal organization, and smoothly transitions to a role that supports the internal group.

A few companies invest in a solid internal usability group during the early phases of institutionalization, but most companies start with a usability consultancy. The consultancy brings an integrated and experienced team of people and a complete set of resources. They can help set up a well-tuned strategy and do most of the work of setting up the infrastructure. Consultants are skilled in supporting change management issues. As outside experts, their advice is often more easily accepted. Also, in the unlikely event the whole initiative fails, consultants are easy and inexpensive to fire. For all these reasons, it makes sense to start with a consultancy.

In my experience at HFI, the cost of an effective initial setup for addressing usability concerns within a large company could be about $500,000 USD just for consultant costs. This level of investment is required to cover the minimum set of activities, documents, and deliverables needed in order to get usability going.

You should select a usability consultancy that has a critical mass of staff, processes, tools, and specialists who can help with the startup tasks and the creation of the infrastructure. You want to select a consultancy with a full infrastructure because you do not want to create a methodology and toolkit from scratch. Also, be sure to select a firm with a good set of training courses so you won't need to build and maintain a suite of courses for your company—this can be a very expensive and time-consuming endeavor.

The consultancy's role changes over time. In the Startup and Setup phases, the consultancy guides the strategy and establishes the infrastructure. The firm may help with the design of one or two showcase projects. In the Organization phase, the consultancy helps with recruiting and supporting the initial projects where the internal staff members are not yet in place, experienced, and confident. During the Long-Term Operations phase, the role changes again. The consultancy should continue to provide training and supplemental support where needed. This supplemental support may take the form of a very high-level consultant who performs audits and provides a second opinion. Or it may take the form of specialists who help with uncommon technologies. The consultancy may also provide lower-level staff to help fill the ranks of usability practitioners. A particular advantage comes if the firm can provide offshore usability support. Done properly, the quality and low cost of an offshore group can make it possible to support all the projects that need usability work.

It is important to select the right consultancy, and this chapter will help you by describing what you should look for. Table 4-1 summarizes the

Table 4-1: *Weighted Criteria for Selecting a Usability Consultancy*

Criteria	Description	Points
Staffing	Has trained and professional usability personnel	17
Completeness of solution	Can provide a complete integrated solution, rather than hiring multiple vendors who specialize in niche areas	16
Domain expertise	Saves time and offers some special insights for your specific domain	11
Methodology	Follows a methodology that has clear activities and deliverables and is appropriate and comprehensive	10
Tools and templates	Already has an infrastructure of tools and templates in place	9
Size and stability	Is large enough to absorb your project requirements	8
Corporate cultural match	Matches or complements your own corporate culture	6
Specializations	Has a wide range of specializations in the field	5
Organizational structure	Has a clear and easy-to-work-with organizational structure	5
Change management ability	Helps you build usability into your organization rather than just providing usability consultancy	5
Quality control and feedback	Has a good quality assurance and process improvement program in place	4
Ongoing training for consultant's staff	Makes a continuous effort to keep staff up-to-date in usability knowledge and practice	4
Total points		**100**

selection criteria and suggests weightings for these items. While it is unlikely that any consultancy will score 100%, try to find a company that comes close. We have included a point system to reflect that some items are more important than others. This rating system should hold well across different organizations, but you may want to adjust the weightings to match your needs and priorities.

Staffing

You should make sure that your consultancy has professional usability engineering staff. (Chapter 12, Staffing, describes the different types of usability engineering skills.)

Some of the consultancy's staff should have advanced degrees in usability engineering. These degrees can go by different names, including the following:

- Software Ergonomics
- Human Factors Engineering
- Engineering Psychology

The staff members may also have backgrounds in cognitive psychology or sensation and perception.

Make sure that the staff members are oriented toward practical design work rather than research. If some staff members publish a lot, make sure that their firm also employs people who do the practical work. They should be familiar with the current research, but they don't have to author it all.

At least some of the staff members should have substantial experience in the field. It typically takes ten years to develop solid competence. Although some of the staff may have less experience than this, a consultancy in which most of the members have only one or two years in the field is not experienced enough to guide you.

Without skilled staff, there will be little value added by the consultancy, no matter how good its infrastructure is. These people must be at the vanguard and become role models for future growth within your organization.

Completeness of Solution

Some companies can provide only pieces of your usability solution—some may only perform usability testing or training, while others may offer expertise in projects or do high-level change management consulting. You can try to piece together a solution, but the parts will not entirely match. Certainly, all good usability consultants have a similar philosophy and work from similar principles. However, even small discrepancies in the interpretation of research or nomenclature can reduce credibility and confuse the internal stakeholders. Therefore, select a consultancy that can provide a complete and integrated solution, including the elements listed below.

- **Support for institutionalization:**
  - *Strategic consulting*—consulting on the strategies for usability within the organization
  - *Expert reviews*—evaluation of existing technology products, such as applications or Web sites, to see what usability problems they contain
  - *Introductory training*—training on the basics of usability
  - *Detailed skill-level training*—training on more detailed skills for in-house usability professionals
  - *Methodological standards*—standards for a user-centered design process
  - *Design standards*—standards for the visual and interaction decisions for projects
  - *Templates and tools to support the standards*—tools to make standards easy to implement
  - *Recruiting of usability practitioners*—help and advice in finding qualified practitioners
- **User-centered design on specific projects:**
  - *High-level user interface design*—consulting expertise in high-level design for critical and showcase projects
  - *Graphic design*—graphic design expertise that dovetails with usability

- ○ *Detailed design and functional specifications*—user requirements from a usability point of view
- ○ *Usability testing*—consulting and help with the design and implementation of standard usability test protocols
- **Ongoing support:**
  - ○ *New research updates*—a strategy for keeping the staff up-to-date on the latest work and research
  - ○ *Usability audits*—periodic audits of standards and processes
  - ○ *Mentoring*—mentoring of both executives and practitioners to advance their expertise

These criteria are very important because the effort required to manage a fragmented solution is significant. Even simple problems like terminology can slow the process. (For example, is the description of the user's workflow called *task design, scenario creation,* or *storyboards?*)

Domain Expertise

The consultant should understand the general domain of your business, but he or she does not need extensive specific domain expertise. However, general expertise in your type of applications is important. For example, if you produce software for chemical engineers, your consultant should have experience with scientific applications. This is an example of high-level domain expertise. If you are in the financial industry, it is important that the consultant have experience with financial products. The consultant does not need to be knowledgeable about your particular type of chemical product offering or financial offering.

Every organization has a particular focus. Examples include systems for manufacturing automobiles, managing time reporting for lawyers, and genetic engineering. These specific domains are very unique, and although it would be helpful to have a consultant who is familiar with your specific domain, it is more important that the consultant have some general domain knowledge and the ability to augment that with exceptional usability expertise. People who select usability consultants often overestimate the importance of specific domain expertise.

Consider how you might choose an accounting firm. It is certainly helpful if your accounting firm has worked in your industry. After all, your industry has some unique conventions and special needs, so a certain level of familiarity with these issues could save days or weeks of time that would otherwise be dedicated to investigation and learning. But when it comes right down to it, the accounting domain is pretty similar across industries. If this were not true, there would be no large accounting firms, and all accounting would be completed by specialty firms focused on narrow vertical markets. You may be better off with a firm that knows your industry less because that firm has better staff or a superior process.

Like accounting, usability work is pretty similar across domains. It does help to know the business—consultants with domain knowledge can save some time and offer some special insights—but having this level of expertise is not the most important factor to consider when choosing a consultancy.

Methodology

Select a consultancy that follows a complete and systematic user-centered development process. This means that the process is fully documented and has specified activities and deliverables that can be modified as needed to meet each new set of project demands. It is also important that the methodology you choose be appropriate and comprehensive.

There are many user-centered design methods available. Dr. Susan Weinschenk developed the InterPhase 5 methodology while with The Weinschenk Consulting Group. HFI has developed its own user-centered development process, which is outlined in Chapter 7. *The Usability Engineering Lifecycle: The Practitioner's Handbook for User Interface Design* by Deborah Mayhew [1999] describes another such process. A brief look at the evolving software usability methodologies would include the following[1]:

- *Gould and Lewis (1985)*—published one of the earliest usability methodologies
- *Manter and Teorey (1988)*—outlined a usability methodology integrated into a standard software development life cycle
- *Nielsen (1992)*—expanded earlier usability principles to ten detailed steps that should be integrated into an overall development plan
- *Schneiderman (1992)*—introduced eight interactive stages for usability considerations across any interactive systems development process
- *Mayhew (1992)*—advanced usability methodology by offering more detailed specifications for integrating iterative usability techniques into the software development cycle

Tools and Templates

User-centered design requires a lot of work, but the amount of effort can be vastly reduced if the consultant has a set of tools and templates that support the process. Templates such as questionnaires for interviews, screeners for usability testing, templates for documenting expert reviews, and usability testing reports are critical to ensure that deliverables are easy to create and standardize. Without these templates in place, the consultant will spend time reinventing everything from scratch. This is expensive and also will extend the project time line.

In addition to the templates, there is significant value in having a set of tools. The consultancy might have remote testing software, a portable or fixed usability testing lab, and software for tasks like cluster analysis of card sort data. Working with tools and templates

---

1. This list is summarized from *Cost-Justifying Usability* [Bias and Mayhew 1994], which presents information on these authoritative methodology texts in more detail. Please consult that source for full bibliographic information for the books listed here.

makes consultants more efficient and the deliverables and results more consistent. But it is even *more* important that you get these tools and templates so that your company can use them in the future. It makes more sense to use a commercial off-the-shelf solution and have it customized to meet your needs than to invest in creating these resources from scratch. You can certainly create your own templates over time, but having a set to start with saves months of effort.

Size and Stability

Many usability consulting firms have only one practitioner or a handful of them and perhaps some additional contractors. These companies can have significant limitations. If you are working on a usability institutionalization program in a large company, your needs might inundate the abilities of quality staff in a small organization. Even if your organization is small, a one- or two-person consultancy group will be quickly overwhelmed by the swings in demands during even one project.

If a consulting firm has eight staff members and you hire all eight staff members for five months, at the end of the project you might find that the firm disappears because it cannot immediately find new work to absorb all of the resources that were released at the end of your project. This situation may be disconcerting because it also means that the same organization will not be there to help later when you have additional needs.

A large firm can provide several people to support your projects and won't collapse when you don't need that support for a while. Larger firms are also generally more stable. The fact that these companies are well established means that they will be more likely to be there for you over time, and they are more likely to have specialists to meet your needs and facilities to support your effort.

Needless to say, it is a serious problem to have a consulting company fold in the middle of your strategy. The time you have spent getting its staff members up to speed on your organization will be lost. If the consulting firm cannot meet your fluctuating needs, you will have to slow down or modify your process to accommodate the limited capacity and capabilities.

Corporate Cultural Match

It is not easy to achieve a perfect fit between corporate cultures. You want to be sure that the consultancy's technical staff will fit with your company's environment. In some situations, it helps to have a strong figure who can walk into a confusing situation and provide order. In others, you may need a usability expert who can work with your team and smoothly create consensus. It is important that the consultants have some flexibility in style. It may be even more important that they can provide different staff with different personalities and working styles to best fit your corporate culture.

Many other special characteristics of organizations need to be considered. In some cases, uncomplimentary cultures present some advantages. For example, a very systematic and controlled culture might need a consultant who can break the mold, be artistic and different. On the other hand, if your organization lacks a systematic process, it helps to have a consultant who can inspire that. But in most cases similarity in cultures is more helpful because it often leads to a more comfortable long-term relationship. If you have a scientific- and engineering-oriented culture, pick a usability firm that has a similar approach. While the consultant will work intensely with you for a relatively short period, there will also be a less concentrated, longer-term relationship. Thus being comfortable with your consultant's organization has value.

Specializations

Hiring a consultancy that has staff with different specializations in the field offers a significant advantage. People who have focused deeply on a given topic can answer questions in an instant.

There are many different types of specialists. Some usability professionals have experience in meeting the exact challenges of specific populations:

- Cross-cultural and multilingual design
- Design for the visually impaired
- Design for children

Some have experience in specific technologies:

- Handheld and wireless
- Telematics
- Voice response
- Web
- Windows applications

Others have experience with specific technical areas and topics:

- Search strategies
- Natural language dialogs
- Representation of large networks

Some staff may have particular experience in different parts of the user-centered design process:

- Interviewing
- Usability testing
- Graphics
- Prototyping

Usability staff also may specialize in certain types of situations and businesses:

- E-commerce
- Intranets
- Shrink-wrapped software

Having consultants with a wide range of experiences at your disposal allows you to draw on solutions from many contexts. For example, someone with cross-cultural design expertise would take one look and notice that your command abbreviation "S" may mean "save" in English, but it will mean "exit" (*sortie*) in French.

Organizational Structure

Look for a consulting firm with the necessary staff to fit with your organization. If you are a small organization, it may not be difficult to manage all the usability work that is occurring simultaneously. If you are larger organization, your consultancy may also need to offer a business manager to handle the contractual relationships, an accounting contact to handle payment issues, and a separate legal person to handle nondisclosure and contractual issues. For large-scale efforts, you have to deal with more people than just the usability consultants.

There will always be a primary usability lead and perhaps some additional usability staff on the team. But it helps a lot to have an escalation channel separate from the usability lead. Having only the usability lead as a contact can make it embarrassing and challenging to communicate when difficulties arise in the consulting engagement, especially if the usability lead has created the problem!

Change Management Ability

The consultant must provide high-level strategic guidance in the organizational process. Organizations must often realign to support a user-centered design process and almost always have to manage resistance to change. The consultant will actually provide assistance in change management. **Change management** refers to making changes in a planned and systematic way in order to make the transition to new processes easy and effective. This kind of guidance should include pointing out pitfalls, helping to identify and manage specific areas and people in need of special attention, and assisting with opening communication channels. The consultant should directly support the organizational process and have lots of examples, case histories, and research to substantiate his or her position.

Select a consultant who will help you meet your essential political goals and will defend your best interests, even at his or her own expense—one who will "stand in front of a freight train" for you. The consultant should have the ability to talk as a peer to anyone, at any level of the organization.

For some organizations, change management may be an important but not critical factor in the success of the usability implementation. For other organizations with a history of change management issues or with highly charged changes already under way, effective change management might be a "make or break" factor in implementing usability.

Quality Control and Feedback

Some organizations rely on the skills of a single practitioner to ensure the quality of usability process deliverables. There is often no standard process, review, or oversight. This is like the early days of programming when the work was done in a garage by a master programmer. If he or she was good enough, the code would work, but there was usually no concept of a separate and formal quality assurance process. The only concept of process improvement was trial and error.

Look for a consultancy that has good methods to ensure quality. Is there a method of certifying staff quality and knowledge? Is there a review process for deliverables? Is there a process for gathering feedback about the quality of the design and results and improving from lessons learned?

Make sure the consultancy has a systematic user-centered methodology and actually follows it. This ensures a more reliable application of design. This methodology is the minimum. Seek a consultancy that engages in ongoing process improvement. Provisions for quality assurance and process improvement indicate a more mature organization that will give you far better service and support.

Ongoing Training for the Consultancy's Staff

Earlier in the chapter, I mentioned that the consultancy should provide training for you, but the other side of that criterion concerns how the firm keep *its* staff current. New ideas, insights, methods, and technologies develop within the field all the time. If the company does not gather and disseminate these insights, you will not benefit from current best practices.

It is good to hire a consultancy that makes a continuous investment in improving its staff members' knowledge and practice. Chapter 6 lists some of the critical conferences in the field that at least some of the consulting firm's staff should attend. Each of these conferences provides insights that will be valuable to your projects. There is also a continuous stream of useful books, articles, and e-communications.

For example, usability specialists used to think that the optimal limit on menu size was either 7 (plus or minus 2) or 10 items [Miller 1956]. More recent research suggests that the optimal menu size is more like 16–36 items, as long as they are presented in groups of not more than 10 items each [Paap and Roske-Hofstrand 1986]. The usability field is constantly adding new principles and methods. Select a consultancy that keeps up-to-date by ensuring that its staff members attend conferences and classes and read the latest material; its team will help you have the best and most current usability engineering program.

A good usability consultancy is invaluable in helping your organization transition to an efficient and thorough user-centered design process. It is worth spending some additional time in screening consulting firms early in your institutionalization effort to make sure that you choose the one with the most appropriate capabilities for your organization. The next chapter provides insights into how you can create a practical strategy for your efforts that includes the activities and resources you have begun to formulate.

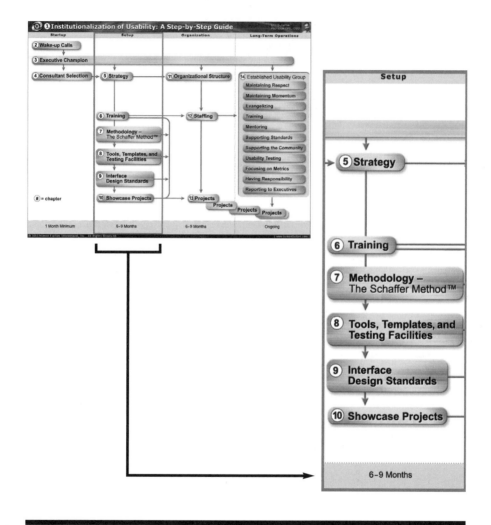

Part II

Setup

The Setup phase establishes the infrastructure needed to complete efficient and professional usability work. Certainly, you could hire some usability staff members and put them into project teams. But completing this phase creates the difference between a real institutionalization effort and unprofessional puttering. Without an effective strategy, training, methodology, facilities, tools, templates, and standards, a usability practitioner is unlikely to be successful and efficient.

In the Setup phase, you create a strategic plan that includes specifically sequenced steps, resources, and activities. The strategic plan helps you build an infrastructure to support ongoing usability work. This infrastructure includes training for everyone, which provides an understanding of usability as well as specific skills for the design team. You develop a user-centered design methodology, integrated with the general system development life cycle. A user-centered process makes the design of the user taskflows and experiences the first priority.

You also create a set of reusable questionnaires and templates, decide what facilities and equipment you need, and develop interface design standards. The Setup phase is about building the infrastructure so that ongoing user-centered design can be completed in an efficient, repeatable, and professional manner.

Quite a few components and interactions are included in the Setup phase. The methodology must work with internal processes, and the standards must work with the technology and the business objectives. With all these complex elements to address, you can't expect everything to work out smoothly the first time. That's why the showcase project is strongly recommended—to work out the kinks in the process and prove that it all works.

Chapter 5

Strategy

> Create a strategic plan that is just a few pages long. It should outline the specific steps, resources, and staff responsibilities.

> Getting this plan right is critical. It is a very complex puzzle, specific to your situation.

> Select and sequence activities to optimize practicality, efficiency, and support for cultural change.

> Bootstrap the usability effort. The benefits of the small early activities often can fund the larger tasks of establishing infrastructure and an internal team.

People often think of developing strategies as a time-consuming academic exercise that involves the creation of complex planning documents. But for the institutionalization of usability, your strategy can be devised more quickly and simply. You might be able to formulate your company's strategy in a few hours. You may want to try it after reading this chapter or perhaps after you have finished the whole book. In a larger organization, creating a strategy could take a bit longer because you may need to build consensus and fine-tune the direction before you begin drafting the strategy. Many of the topics in this chapter are discussed in more detail in other chapters. The focus of this chapter is how to think about each area in the context of your strategic plan.

Your strategy does not have to be a long document—if it's longer than six pages, it is probably at the wrong level and is a detailed plan, not a strategy. Figure 5-1 illustrates a sample strategy document.

Sample Strategy—Unisom Pvt., Ltd. Usability Institutionalization Strategy for January–June			
Projects	**Organized By**	**Details**	**Cost**
Training Plan	DESEC Training	Four open presentations of the Basic Usability Course (two in Washington office, one in Colorado, and one in Texas). Schedule ASAP.	About 40K
	TNF Development T. Smith, Lead	Two presentations of Web Design class (Washington office). Openings for 25 people per course. Schedule ASAP.	20K
Methodology	TNF Development T. Smith, Lead	Purchase The Schaffer Method and integrate with current RUP process. Target completion by Feb 1.	30K
Facilities, Tools, and Templates	TNF Purchasing F. Chavan, Lead	Agreements to use testing facilities in Washington and Texas. Target completionby Feb 1.	None until used
	TNF Development T. Smith, Lead	Prepare customized set of testing and contextual inquiry questionnaires customized to our environ-ment. Target completion by April 1.	40K
Standards	TNF Development T. Smith, Lead	Develop customized interface standard to cover our public Web presence, extranet, and intranet. Target completion by March 15.	140K
Showcase Projects	T. Lam, Development Manager	New expense reporting system for intranet. To be completed as Showcase Project. Expected start—June 1.	About 175K
	S. Chandra, Development Manager	Public Web site module for new member regis-tration. To be completed as Showcase Project. Expected start—June 15.	About 150K
Organization and Staffing	Office of the President	Create initial concept for organizational structure and staffing levels. Target completion by May 15 for presentation at Director's Conference.	About 25K
	Personnel Department D. Lang, Lead	Recruit head of central usability team. Target—start by April 1, sooner if feasible.	About 130K per year

Figure 5-1: *Sample Strategy for Institutionalizing Usability*

Once the strategy is complete, the usability staff can develop the detailed planning.

This chapter indicates some of the key considerations and tradeoffs you will need to be aware of when carefully composing a strategy. No simple formula works in all environments, and it's important to get your strategy right because a poor strategic plan can doom your institutionalization effort.

What to Consider When Developing the Strategic Plan

While it may take two years to complete your overall institutionalization effort, your strategic plan should cover the next 6 to 12 months. It should identify necessary staff, financial support, and the activities appropriate for your environment. You should also put your strategy in a sequence that optimizes efficiency and process acceptance and includes a set of decision points where you will assess the progress and value of the effort. Your strategy must identify the planned activities, time frame, resources, and responsible entities in your organization and should address the following questions.

- What sequence of usability initiatives will work best? Although some steps must be completed before others, you have choices on some of the sequence decisions you make.

- Have you considered your environment? How does your organization affect the way you implement the institutionalization of usability?

- What are your most pressing concerns and objectives? As you begin the process of institutionalizing usability, you can have it unfold in a way that meets your most important issues.

- Are there people or organizations that most need to get on board? Pockets of resistance exist in every organization. Identifying yours and building them into your strategic plan is critical.

The strategy essentially describes *who* will be responsible in your organization and *what* they will be doing. This concept seems simple, but the decisions you make have significant implications. The following sections cover the main considerations involved in selecting the *who* and *what* for your strategy. Your usability consultant may be able to help you think about these issues and form the best strategy for your environment.

A Proactive Organization

As you start the institutionalization effort, it is essential to set up a proactive effort. It is easy to start putting out the numerous fires of poor usability and to have a small group of dedicated staff working to fix the tidal wave of bad designs, one by one. Be forewarned—this approach is guaranteed to fail. It is like having doctors administer to all the health needs of the community, from taking temperatures and applying bandages to transporting patients and performing surgery. The medical community can't work that way, and neither can your usability staff.

The medical community has paramedics, nurses, and physician's assistants to help with the range of activities. For your company's strategy, you need to build a similar set of facilities to create a proactive organization. This is the only way to ensure routine usability.

Coordinating Internal Staff and Consultants

In Chapter 4, we covered why to consider using an outside usability consultant and how to choose one. Even with all the value that a consultant can bring to an organization, internal staff remains invaluable. Using internal staff costs less than hiring local consultants, but there are far more advantages than just cost. Internal staff members are the only people able to fully focus on the business content and strategy from within the company. They can learn the subject matter deeply. This means they can be more efficient in design work. They can also develop a set of instruments and procedures that really fit perfectly with the issues your company must manage. For example, if they are in the medical field, they are aware of the latest FDA requirements. If they are in customer service, they know the history of issues with workstation and voice response system integration. They know what to attend to in the next release. Internal staff members are the most familiar with customers and the organization.

These staff members also have an advantage because they work in the organization on a long-term basis. They have established relationships with employees and groups within the company that are not involved in usability. And perhaps most importantly, they know the opinion leaders and the sources of power in the organization. They can therefore reach a level of consensus and buy-in that cannot be achieved with consultants. It is too easy to tell a consultant, "Yes, user-centered design will be accomplished now," and then ignore the whole issue the next week when the consultant is gone. The internal group is in a unique position to deeply ingrain the usability perspective into the organization.

Organizations vary a lot, so it is vital that your strategy fits your company culture. For example, some companies may be accustomed to having consultants work closely but independently, others may want a consultant to just coach them briefly, and others may prefer to do all the work with in-house staff.

As you strategize about how to use external consultants along with internal staff, make sure the consulting firm is flexible about what kind and how much work its staff completes compared with your company's internal staff. For example, your organization may not have a lot of internal staff time to devote to developing interface design standards. In this instance, the internal staff should spend a limited amount of time working in the standard committee and reviewing documents in order to make the process efficient. The consulting firm should do the bulk of the standards development, but the internal staff should always make the final decisions (based on training and with the consultants' guidance).

Another organization that requires more internal ownership may need to work differently with the consulting firm. For that group, one of the consulting firm's staff may need to be onsite within the organization. In this scenario, the consulting practitioner would not actually create the standard but would work as a coach and as a resource. This might take longer and may cost more, but for some organizations it is the right approach because they will internalize the standard, own it, and use it.

The combination of consultant staff and internal staff needs to be part of your strategy and needs to fit within your culture.

Consultant and Internal Group Mix

By Todd Gross, Ph.D., Director—Corporate Statistics and Human Factors, Medtronic MiniMed

At Medtronic MiniMed, we have used a mix of in-house and outside resources to complete our human factors projects. Outside consulting offers several benefits. Consultants can focus on our project exclusively, whereas in-house personnel often must juggle multiple projects. Consulting firms also often have greater resources and expertise to dedicate to a project. This allows them to complete the projects more quickly and with more polished output than we might be able to do ourselves.

Another benefit of outside consultants is that they bring a fresh perspective to the project. There is great value in taking the extra 20%, 30%, or even 50% of the time to really take the project through and to present it in a way that is valuable. There's something about hearing it from an outside entity—the good news sounds better and the bad news has greater credibility than when in-house personnel present it. It's sort of like if a date tells you that you dress funny, you might give that greater credence than if your mother tells you the same thing.

In my experience, outside consultants and internal staff can provide a powerful alliance to promote the use of human factors knowledge throughout the organization. I like the idea of continuing to have a department that provides core resources. And I think that long range, we need to have that internal core. But one of the things I have noticed is that it's important to have a consultant and internal group mix, especially for a company like Medtronic MiniMed, where we make devices with a broad range of human factors issues. Some of our devices are purely mechanical and others are electronic, with both hardware and software interface issues. We found that in some cases, we can't expect to have all the expertise we need in all those areas. If we want to really have the biggest impact we can in terms of human factors work and usability, sometimes it's better to go to an outside firm that has expertise in that area.

My vision for the future is that we have a core group in-house that can do the bulk of the work but then also recognize when it is necessary to get some outside help. The consultant may have the skills necessary to develop mental models of the tasks, to go out in the user population and understand what the taskflow is before the product even occurs. This is important work. We are just beginning to develop our core resources in the area of human factors—we have some challenges in terms of devoting the resources necessary to make the process more mature. The outside consultant can bolster our efforts with additional resources, thereby taking our projects and the entire usability program to the next level.

The Importance of Sequence

This book presents phases and activities for institutionalizing usability, but most companies modify this process somewhat. As you develop your strategy, be sure to consider the sequence of activities that will make the most sense for your environment.

Many logical connections are built into the institutionalization methodology described in this book. For instance, keep the following sequences in mind.

- Have your strategy in place before the infrastructure setup; otherwise, you will spend money in an inefficient and uncoordinated way.

- Have standards in place before starting projects; otherwise, you will create a larger installed base of noncompliant designs.
- Get the upfront design process working before doing usability testing so that testing can fine-tune reasonable designs instead of documenting designs that are not even close to correct.
- Finalize your organizational design before you start the hiring process so you can be sure to hire staff with the right skills and abilities.

These interdependencies are important and should always be considered when planning your strategy. It is also important to use the sequence to maintain flexibility. Similar to a chess game, it is unwise to move in a way that removes options unnecessarily.

As an example of the value of considering sequence, let's use the idea of when to hire usability staff. It's often better to delay hiring usability staff until a bit later in the process. This is partly because hiring is an action that is difficult and expensive to change. As the early stages of institutionalization unfold, you may change your view of staffing issues: the type and number of staff members, their skill levels, and their personalities. Therefore, it's better to get the infrastructure in place and do at least one showcase project before hiring full-time usability staff. Your staffing requirements may change significantly upon the completion of such a project, so you may want to delay hiring until then. There could be cases in which this process should proceed differently. For example, your company may already have had a usability team in place from the beginning. Therefore, your strategy will need to be adjusted accordingly.

Reacting to Past Events

Many organizations have had bad experiences with consultants. This can make it difficult for the organization to work with a usability consultant. The consultant may say he or she is different, but the organization may have heard the same claim from the previous consultant.

The most critical insight for this type of situation is to go about the process more slowly. If you have a negative history with outside consultants, you may need to start with very small projects. Take time to gain trust and put the bad experience well in the past. The staff may also need much more explanation. There is never a time when people should take usability recommendations on trust. They should always be given the full rationale and research data behind each recommendation. Allow extra time for this.

Another past event to watch out for is whether the organization has had a difficult wake-up call. This otherwise negative experience can be used as a resource that provides momentum for change in the organization. However, challenges like this can also create too much drive. Overall, it is best to avoid strategies that are driven by a sense of panic. They rarely work well in the long term. If you have this situation, avoid taking on lots of projects. Instead, select a couple of key programs and make sure they are completed successfully.

Targets of Opportunity

The greatest drivers for differences in strategy are the tactical opportunities that exist. It is important to establish a plan that takes advantage of the organization's current activities. It makes sense to shift the sequence of institutionalization activities to take advantage of these types of events.

You might find that you can get training in conjunction with another company in your area, so training might be moved to meet this schedule.

You might find that you are installing a revised system development methodology. This is a great time to add a user-centered process to supplement the new method. In this way, you can train staff on the new method, instead of having them learn the system-centric method and then learn about user-centered design separately.

You might select a showcase project because it is visible, or because the staff members are very interested in usability, or because the project is small and manageable and needs to start at the right time for the usability initiative.

Perhaps you have an opportunity to hire a very skilled usability specialist who is a good fit for your culture. Usability staff with skills and compatibility are very hard to find and may be on the market only for weeks. So if unique opportunities are present, mold your strategy to hire sooner.

Clearly, as you establish your strategy, you must shape it to your opportunities and also expect some fine-tuning as new opportunities arise.

Slower Can Be Better

Achieving a successful institutionalization of usability program requires time and patience. There is an uncomfortable joke in aviation that captures this principle quite well. A plane called the "V-Tailed Doctor Killer" has a funny tail design, but more to the point it is a powerful and complicated aircraft. Many doctors have the money to buy such a machine, but they do not have the time or experience to use it safely. They can fly it under normal and comfortable circumstances, but in more dangerous and pressure-filled moments, they lose control.

It is the same with a usability effort. You can buy a complete usability infrastructure and set of activities. You can implement training, methodology, standards, tools, projects, and hiring. It takes a great deal of effort and money to put these elements in place, but until the organization has had time to digest each intervention and each component of the infrastructure, there is little value. It is easy to bite off too much and then think you are well fed. Take your time in implementing usability, and build that time into your strategy.

Phasing in Design Standards

In your strategic plan, make sure you get interface design standards in place early. Good design standards are so valuable that they can be justified almost any time there will be significant and ongoing development. It is as though you can hear a clock ticking when there are no standards. Certainly standards save development time—there is a real increase in expenses if developers must spend time reinventing the wheel. Also, the developers do not have the time, skill, or attention to dedicate to a design that a standards team has. Therefore, the designs are almost sure to be suboptimal. But the biggest concern is that all those current projects that are completed without standards will create a growing set of noncompliant screens.

Without a standard, you will develop an increasing body of noncompliant screens. These screens must then be modified to bring them into compliance. This is a daunting task, and no company ever seems to do it all at once. Instead, noncompliant designs are grandfathered in. They are brought into compliance with the standard only when they are being revised as part of some renovation or enhancement program. This makes the conversion less daunting and spreads the cost over years. It seems to be the rational thing to do, but it is still quite costly to just let developers keep churning out nonstandard designs while delaying standards development.

Besides the costs due to the eventual need to convert the designs, a psychological cost makes it tougher to create standards. It is difficult to develop standards with a committee that represents an installed base of noncompliant and diverse designs. You can see each committee member judging the concepts based on how close they are to his or her own designs or the designs of his or her department. These committee members cannot see the ergonomic quality of designs, and they cannot interpret the value of the design to the company; they are simply entrenched in defending their past decisions.

These are hard groups to work with. You end up having to painstakingly take apart the past designs one by one. Typically, you have to show the ergonomic problems with the old designs, and the people involved have to go through the process of accepting that they created an imperfect design and realizing that these designs need changes.

Providing a training class for the committee members smoothes this process immeasurably. With training, the members can see the problems with their designs themselves. But the larger the installed base, the more staff members have a vested attachment to the designs, and the more they have a visceral resistance to making changes. There is no question that you avoid making unnecessary changes with past design convention. But people develop powerful arguments for very poor designs because it is hard for them to accept that their designs need to be changed.

Key Groups for Support or Resistance

The institutionalization of usability requires a set of discrete activities and resources, but the key to success does not lie in these accomplishments. It lies in the understanding and beliefs of the people within the organization. It is not unusual for companies to spend six figures on a usability testing lab, only to see it sit unused. Without the acceptance of usability as a focus of concern by the people in the organization, there will be no real success.

The people in your organization break into a number of key groups from the viewpoint of institutionalization. First, there are the early adopters, who are easily excited about usability and almost instantly grasp the concept, methods, principles, process, and value. The earliest stages of the institutionalization effort need to focus on identifying these people and getting them on board because they will provide the early momentum. As time goes on, you will need to worry about keeping them motivated and preventing them from feeling too frustrated with the pace of the overall organization. If they become bitter, they will alienate others, so keep them seeing successes.

A second key group is the power structure within the company. In a sense, the progress of institutionalization is wholly reflected in this group's level of understanding and appreciation. As user-centered design becomes a given from the executive suite, impediments will melt, resources will appear, and success will be assured. If the executives are indifferent, long-term success is essentially impossible. Reaching these players is key. Put effort into including them in the design process (as experts in strategic direction and brainstorming), communicating successes, and providing education. You do not need these leaders to do the design work, but they should help you work on the organization's process of design.

When executives get involved in design, they follow a number of patterns. They may attempt to micromanage the entire process or to single-handedly reinvent the entire usability engineering profession and literature. Other executives may drop into the design process periodically and make recommendations. This is usually quite

---

Executive Support for Usability within AT&T

By Feliça Selenko, Principal Technical Staff Member, AT&T

In an employee message to the people of AT&T, Dave Dorman, AT&T CEO, states, "AT&T has an important initiative under way to dramatically improve our 'customer lifecycle' processes. The intent of this effort is to drive higher levels of customer satisfaction and retention, and differentiate AT&T from the rest of our industry. By removing errors and the resulting rework, we reduce cycle time, improve customer satisfaction and reduce our costs of doing business." That sentiment is reflected in every set of executive goals and objectives I have seen this year, that is, optimizing the customer experience is always one of the most important goals/objectives.

Although AT&T executives are using the term *customer experience,* which is broader than usability, goals/objectives focusing on the automation of manual processes, optimizing the customer's self-serve experience via easy-to-use Web tools, and removing errors from processes and interactions to reduce rework and improve cycle times are all aspects of the customer experience impacted by usability engineering.

---

detrimental, but the worst situation is the executive who hands down design edicts from on high. These are the people who want to see "a big red area at the top" or "a tree view at the left."

These executives are usually so powerful that the design team feels forced to follow their orders precisely. Such an executive becomes an all-powerful design constraint. The design team already has enough constraints, and these types of edicts rarely have a positive impact. Executives need to reinforce the need for user-centered design and the value of optimizing user experience, performance, and design consistency, but executives should never specify a design feature. Even with great experience and training, it is quite difficult for a consultant to select any substantive design decision that can be mandated in every situation, so executives should certainly not attempt to do so.

A third important group is the people who are against usability, or the "naysayers." It might seem odd to think there could possibly be people like this today, but there are. Down deep, they do not want to lose control of the design process. They want to continue to enjoy the comfort of designing things *they* like, without needing to validate that the users can understand, use, or appreciate the result. There is a joyful freedom gained from just spewing forth elegant code. There is an unpleasant messiness in being forced to meet the inconsistent and ambiguous needs of users. Naysayers won't admit to this type of thinking, but it is often what really happens down deep.

Naysayers can come from different groups. Marketing staff members might think things will go well if they make sites that wiggle and dazzle users (although users often consider such sites "sales-y" and disreputable). Graphic artists might want to concentrate almost wholly on the beauty of the design and not worry about whether it can be navigated and operated easily. Systems coders might want to use the easiest technological route or perhaps the latest and coolest technological innovation.

These naysayers won't say, "It is fun to refer to user needs and limitations as we design." Instead, they will suggest that systematic user-centered design will "take too much time." Expect them to question the ROI of usability work. (In response, you might ask them if they have ever seen an ROI calculation for having a database designed by professionals instead of by amateurs.) Naysayers may suggest that, because their design intuition is so good, they can create better user interfaces than the ones based on ergonomic principles and user-centered design. The users will certainly like their designs more, these folks will claim. They will suggest that good usability cannot be achieved within technical constraints. If you point them to problems in past designs, they will often reference past technical constraints that were just recently solved by new technology.

Your strategy must eventually address these naysayers. They will listen a bit to proclamations by executives. But they will think to themselves—and also act—as if usability is just the management buzzword of the month. They will pay a bit of lip service and then try to forget it. They will pay a little attention to presentations that demonstrate the value of usability in pilot projects and a bit more attention to presentations that include testimonials from other naysayers who say they saw value and practicality in the user-centered design process.

But there is one strategy that works best. Most of these naysayers will be problem solvers by nature. They will love to solve the most complex development challenges, and they will feel effective when they can break through these challenges and succeed. A transition is possible when these people become involved in the puzzle of user-centered design: When they get wrapped up in finding a way to meet a customer need, they will find that usability is fun. No amount of ROI calculation or explanation will do it. They need to see that usability offers a whole *new* set of fun puzzles that the naysayers can successfully solve.

The final key group includes the masses in the development community—the mainstream developers. Once a strong core group is established to support usability, the members of that core group must begin the process of evangelizing and mentoring the other developers. It takes some time because there are many mainstream developers, and they change slowly. But institutionalization is established only when this mass of developers has been reached. They will be swept up in new projects that apply usability practices. They will also benefit from training and presentations. The mass of developers can also be reached by a set of online methods and tools presented on a company's intranet. Finally, consider including usability as a part of your training program.

Training

While training is not a magic pill, it is a major pillar of the institutionalization effort. You may need several levels of training—for more information, see Chapter 6. Training provides widespread awareness of usability issues and transfers a crucial element of motivation in the early stages of institutionalization. It can also be used to educate executives and evangelize the value of usability.

Training provides skills for developers who must participate in user-centered design. It is true that the fine points of usability engineering seem to be best shared by mentoring, but without training in the basics, the mentoring process is long and frustrating. Skills-level training is really required.

Methodology and Infrastructure

It is common to see companies hire a few usability people and toss them into the design environment. It is like deciding that you want to have metal weapons and hiring a few metal workers. Certainly, they can set up a few huts with hand-driven furnaces and can begin work with a hammer and anvil. But if you want efficiency and quality, you need to build a modern factory—*then* toss the metal workers into the factory and you can expect good results.

Without a user-centered design methodology, the development team members will end up working tactically. They will think of some of the right things to do, and they will have a positive impact, but a systematic approach is more thorough and more efficient. It therefore makes sense to fit a user-centered process to your current development life cycle. Do this early because time spent without a structured process is likely to be inefficient.

Once you've chosen a methodology, you can move toward establishing a toolkit that supports the methodology. Facilities, tools, and templates make work on the usability engineering process even more efficient. These "modern machines" lead to quality and efficiency. Chapter 7 provides more information on methodology, while Chapter 8 provides details on facilities, tools, and templates.

The Project Path

Selecting the projects to work on first is one of the largest decisions in the strategic plan. Obviously, you must select a project that is just starting so you can demonstrate the whole process. You should also select a project that is of manageable size and duration. It helps little to have a showcase project that isn't completed for years.

It is equally important to select a project that has significant usability objectives. Find a project with lots of users to whom user experience and performance is important. Chapter 10 covers in detail what to look for when selecting a showcase project.

Levels of Investment

Usability institutionalization, infrastructure, projects, and staffing are not free. It costs less in the long run to complete designs with the right methods and tools, but in the short run, an investment is required. It is valuable to calculate the ROI for implementing usability within your organization. Know the specific ways that usability will pay off.

The investment in usability can be staged and progressive. For example, in my experience, the investment in a planned wake-up call can be quite small: $25,000 to 50,000 USD covers any reasonable expert review or usability test. The cost of the initial setup of a usability program for a large company by a consultant is typically about $500,000. The cost of establishing a group and supporting it might be $1 million to $3 million annually.[1] So, starting a usability program is a progressive process: Each step should provide confidence to go ahead with the next level of investment, and each step should fund the next.

Your attempts to make usability routine will create significant change throughout your company. A practical, high-level strategy will create the organization necessary to bring your decision making to the next level. This is the transition from a piecemeal and immature usability capability to a mature and well-managed process. The next chapter provides more details for the training element of your strategy.

---

1. This figure, along with the others in this paragraph, is based on HFI's 20 years of experience with hundreds of clients across thousands of user-centered design projects.

Chapter 6

Training

> Training is an effective way to promote usability and ensure that key staff members have the required skills.

> Provide knowledge training to educate most staff members about the importance of the process of usability. It is possible to train hundreds of people in just half a day.

> Provide skills training to development staff members who will be doing interface design work. Instruct them on how to do usability work throughout the cycle of development. It is possible to train dozens of people in three to ten days.

> Encourage the most highly trained staff members to become certified.

> Use the sample training plan in this chapter as the basis for your own plan.

In the institutionalization process, training is both powerful and comfortable. Training is powerful in that it enables sharing insights and achieving shifts in perspective. It is also comfortable because it makes these changes possible without the expense and potential embarrassment of learning while performing actual project work.

The school of hard knocks is a miserable substitute for organized, research-based instruction.

Classes also provide a portal to the literature in the field. There is a billion dollars' worth of research in usability, but it could take a lifetime to read and digest the material that applies just to design. Usability training, like any other educational experience, is a way to get a distillation of the literature—it provides the key insights, principles, facts, and models. If you start the process of institutionalizing usability without training, you will soon find yourself back to design by the school of hard knocks and intuition.

This chapter describes the types of training available and clarifies how training can fit into your overall program. I discuss certification programs and outline a sample training program you can use as a basis for planning your own program. For simplicity and consistency, the examples in this chapter are from HFI, but many other qualified companies and schools provide similar classes (e.g., Nielsen Norman Group, User Interface Engineering, and Deborah J. Mayhew and Associates).

Types of Training

There are two distinct types of training: knowledge training and skills training. In **knowledge training**, participants don't learn to complete a development activity; instead, they gain an appreciation of the need for usability engineering, understand what it is about, and can identify the types of tasks required. With **skills training**, the participants get a good basis for doing actual tasks. They learn what to do and how to do it, and they get to practice it: how to accomplish a task analysis, detailed design review, or usability test. They may need some coaching to get comfortable with the task and fine-tune their skills, but they will have the basic capabilities after completing the skills training.

The Difference between Knowledge and Skills Training

By Dr. Phil Goddard, Director of Training and Certification,
Human Factors International

There are two types of long-term memory: there's declarative memory and there's procedural memory. Declarative memory is a repository for facts—things that you learn about, that you can recite—it's information about things. The other memory repository is procedural memory. Procedural memory stores procedures or processes that you perform or do, and once learned they become automatic and are done unconsciously. In fact, you can't describe them verbally; you often have to struggle to describe them and resort to hand waving.

Expertise requires both knowledge and skill. For example, consider riding a bike—with a little knowledge (rest both hands on the bars, maintain steady speed, keep your feet on the pedals) and lots of practice, you learn how to do it—automatically. Once you've created the procedure for bike riding, it's ready for use anytime. So at the core, knowledge is often a combination of factual information and procedural skill that must be developed over time to result in expertise.

When developing a training program, we should recognize as user-centered designers that we can state factually some things we learn about design. For example, left alignment of all field labels and edit fields on a screen reduces the visual complexity of a page. But there are certain kinds of knowledge that aren't factual—they're more procedural—like performing a usability test. How to perform an effective test that doesn't give away the answer to a specific question, how to actually practice active listening—these things need to be learned over a period of time and assimilated, and sometimes they're just things that take more time to learn.

You have to have both skills training and knowledge training if you want your training program to be powerful.

Knowledge Training

Knowledge training in usability does not have to take a long time. A single day of training is enough to convey the importance of usability and the scope of activities needed. For example, a half-day knowledge training class on Web usability can cover the basics (see Table 6-1). Because knowledge training does not require the level of close interaction and mentoring of skills training, large classes can be as effective as smaller ones. This is especially important if you need to train many people. While the course participants will not be ready to complete usability engineering work after knowledge training, they will better appreciate its importance, and a broad-based appreciation helps the successful implementation of usability.

The best way to ensure a successful institutionalization effort is to get organizational support and acceptance. Knowledge training directly conveys the value of usability engineering and the user-centered design process and provides a baseline of acceptance throughout the organization. The knowledge training does not have to identify every activity and skill needed. It is much more about connecting with people's experiences and getting them to see how usability is an essential tool and can be a key competitive differentiator for their organization. A knowledge training class is a very efficient, organized, and focused method for conveying this understanding. If employees do not have this type of training, the usability staff must convey the same information and understanding on an ad hoc basis. It takes a large amount of time to explain this individually and is inefficient and impractical.

A good knowledge class identifies the overall process of user-centered design and illustrates the value of standards, a good navigational structure, and good detailed design. It does not try to demonstrate all the design principles and research-based recommendations, but it shows enough to ensure that participants understand that usability is not just common sense and should not be approached with anything less than a professional and systematic attitude.

Knowledge training can help make key transitions deep in the psyche of the organization. The entire staff needs to learn how usability is really the way to manifest the strategy from marketing. Everyone

Table 6-1: *Objectives of the HFI Half-Day "Basics of Web Usability" Knowledge Training Class*

This Topic . . .	Will Help You . . .
Usability—the business imperative	Know when to use usability methods and how they benefit users
Information architecture	Organize content and functions so users will find them
Site and page navigation	Select the right site and page navigation model for your users
Writing for the Web	Write text that people can scan or will enjoy reading
Using color effectively	Add depth to your design by using good color principles
Standards and consistency	Consider using a standard to increase design consistency
Usability step by step	Create a usability project plan
How to keep getting better	Increase your skills

needs to learn how usability engineers ensure that the brand values are reflected in the design. Knowledge training can dispel myths, such as the idea that usability engineering goes counter to marketing or graphic design goals. Knowledge training can help move the development organization from design by opinions and superstitions into a systematic and scientific practice.

Who Should Get Knowledge Training?

The usability engineers should certainly receive knowledge training, but in addition, three groups especially benefit from this type of training: executives, members of the systems community, and new employees.

Executives benefit from knowledge training because while they do not need to be able to do a task analysis or complete interviews, they must understand what usability is about. They have to make informed decisions about funding and support the usability staff in the hard choices. Without this type of training, many executives won't have a basic understanding of usability and an appreciation of its importance. While this type of training is not always enough to instill a deep, gut-level commitment to usability, it should have a meaningful impact.

The second target group is the systems community. There are lots of different players within this community, including business owners, product managers, operations personnel, marketing staff, developers, and so on. Different organizations have different types of key staff, so your training program should have the goal of creating a core group of people who understand usability as a primary objective. Regardless of which group you target as the most crucial, the knowledge must permeate the organization. Once this objective is complete, there will always be a few people in every important design meeting who will expect usability to be addressed systematically, scientifically, and as an essential success factor.

It's also important to be sure that new hires are aware of the value of usability. Many new staff members may not know about usability, and knowledge training ensures that they understand the focus on and the importance of usability in the organization.

Although all these groups need to hear a similar message, it is a good idea to customize the presentation to best meet the needs and mindset of each group.

Skills Training

If usability testing were the only thing involved in skills training, this training would be straightforward. But much more is involved than just testing: Skills training needs to provide the ability to participate in the entire cycle of development. There are key usability initiatives to complete at every stage, and this training must support a range of activities, from analyzing the existing site or application to conceptual, navigational, and detailed design.

When you look at the scope of what must be learned, it may seem daunting. In fact, it *is* daunting. Figure 6-1, which outlines course

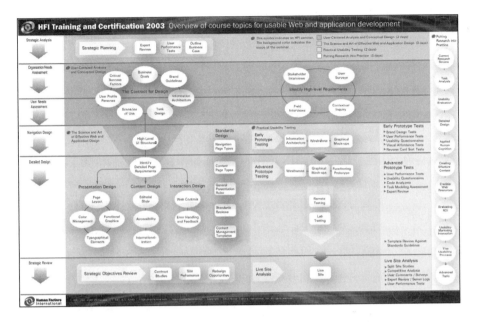

Figure 6-1: *Training Chart: Examples of What Is Taught in Skills Classes to Provide a Solid Level of Training*[1]

topics in the core HFI Web and application development skills training classes, gives you a sense of the scope and complexity of usability skills. Going through a training program provides a foundation, but for most people it takes more than just a training program to become competent at all these activities, given real-world constraints, challenges, and time requirements. Most people do best if they have support for their initial work experience. This support may include advanced training or a mentoring program for refining skills. Support programs can be completed before the start of real-world projects, or they can take the form of participation in showcase projects.

It is also important to have follow-up assistance for newly trained staff. It does not matter that the people are dedicated and determined—there is simply little chance for anyone to get everything right the first time. So, just as there are residency programs

---

1. Chart developed by Dr. Phil Goddard, Director of Training and Certification at Human Factors International. For a larger version, please see Appendix.

for physicians, there is a need for continued mentoring for newly trained usability staff.

Who Should Get Skills Training?

While all employees benefit from knowledge training, those who will do the usability work require skills training. In addition, some managers must be able to evaluate the quality of designs and the design process in depth. This requires an advanced level of training. While the executives might not actually design screens, they have to understand the process, philosophy, and design rules to be able to evaluate and support the usability staff. It is wonderful to have managers with very senior usability experience, but it is more likely that usability will be new to the management group. For managers of usability work who have not had extensive experience, a few days of more in-depth training beyond the knowledge training course should be sufficient.

Both small and large organizations need the same types of training. The difference is in how many people need to be trained.

People who work closely with the usability staff on user-related tasks that support the interface design benefit from a few days of skills training. For example, marketing staff must provide strategic and branding direction, technical staff must support the design's implementation, graphic art staff must create the imagery, and business analysts must consider functionality and business rules. There are user representatives who provide insights and organize data gathering with users, as well as those who work in functional roles that surround the usability activities. With a more solid understanding of the design process, these people will be fully helpful, supportive, and understanding of the importance of usability.

It is useful to pick a few of these individuals and put them through the same training that the usability staff receives. Although they will not be actually completing the tasks, they will then have a clear understanding of what the usability engineer is trying to accomplish and will be more effective in working with them.

Some IT staff and developers may be involved in interface design in a serious way. They may not be dedicated usability staff, but often there is not enough usability staff to do all the user-centered design work. These staff members may be asked to do usability-engineering tasks. For lower-budget projects, or in smaller companies, they may have to provide the entire usability effort on their own, or at least with limited support. These people need about five days of training that provides hands-on skills in user-centered design, including user-centered design and analysis, user interface structures, usability detailed design, and user testing.

Some employees become dedicated usability staff and spend most of their work time on usability issues. They may not have degrees in the field, but they usually care a lot, have industry experience, and possess political skills. They need a solid set of practical training skills. A foundation of ten days of training is of value, and the usability staff should have ongoing mentoring and recurrent training that takes place three days per year.

Certification

You may want to consider certification for staff members who have had a professional level of training. Having the trained staff certified helps instill confidence in them; coworkers will be more likely to respect their insights and decisions, knowing that the staff members who are making recommendations have a solid foundation in the field.

Different levels of certification exist in the usability field. There is the certification of a university degree. Several universities and colleges now offer graduate-level degrees in a human factors field, and some of them are specifically for usability and interface design. Some colleges may not offer a degree but combine courses to offer a certificate. This is not the same as certification; it demonstrates only that the person took some courses.

The Human Factors and Ergonomics Society spun off a certification body called the Board of Certification in Professional Ergonomics.

This body grants a certification in general human factors engineering called either a Certified Professional Ergonomist (CPE) or, in accordance with the certificant's choice, a Certified Human Factors Professional (CHFP). This is a good certification program. It is not focused just on software design—it includes the whole gamut of the human factors engineering practice, from cars and weapons systems to consumer products and power plant controls.

In the last ten years, a few companies have started industry certification programs to fill the gap between a graduate degree and just taking a few courses. For example, HFI has the Certified Usability Analyst (CUA) program. This certification program relies on a test specifically focused on software usability issues. This test, which is quite demanding, measures a person's understanding of user-centered design and usability engineering principles. It does not test the ability to work in groups nor even directly sample design skill, but it does validate that the applicant knows a wide range of research, principles, and methods specific to software usability. The test was constructed systematically with item analysis from various test populations. It is available to all and does not require the participant to complete HFI courses.

A Typical Training Plan

Every company has its own training priorities and budget limits. Table 6-2 outlines a sample plan for the first year; you can use this as a starting point. If you work in a large company, you may want to offer each class in-house to your own people. If you work in a small company, you may wish to send a few people to a public course.

Table 6-2: *Sample HFI Training Plan*

Class	Time Commitment	Description
Management Briefing	Four hours	In this knowledge training class, executives get an overview of the basics of user-centered design and lots of case examples, are acquainted with usability as a business imperative, and learn about the institutionalization effort.
Half Day of Basics	Four hours	This class provides knowledge training for the general development community. Class sizes are large to get training to everyone who needs it.
Web Design Course	Three full days	This skills-level training focuses on screen design for usability staff, key development staff, and a few managers.
User-Centered Analysis and Conceptual Design	Two full days	Moving from initial concept to a user interface design is one of the hardest challenges. This skills course covers how to move from concept to design.
Practical Usability Testing	Two full days	This class presents a synthesis of usability testing techniques for the practitioner. This skills course teaches you to choose the right test for any stage of design, from early to advanced prototypes and live sites.
Certification Track	Ten days training and a test	This training is for practitioners who will be the core of the usability effort.

Conferences

In addition to foundational knowledge and skills training classes, it's important to keep the usability staff current. New ideas and insights occur in this field all the time, and new methods and technologies are being developed continuously. If your company does not gather and disseminate these insights, you will not benefit from current best practices. There are three critical conferences in the field, and each provides insights that will be valuable to your projects. Each person on the core usability team should attend at least one conference a year. Each conference is a little different in terms of the types of people who attend, the types of sessions, and the size of the conference. Visit the Web sites to get an overview of what each conference is like.

- Human Factors and Ergonomics Society (www.hfes.org)
- Special Interest Group on Computer-Human Interfaces of the Association for Computing Machinery (SIGCHI) (www.acm.org/sigchi/)
- The Usability Professionals Association (www.upassoc.org)

Making training an integral part of your institutionalization effort not only helps educate your staff but also provides an invaluable level of ongoing consensus and support. Training is one of the most effective resources available to simultaneously enhance the knowledge, skills, enthusiasm, and commitment of your organization. The next chapter outlines the essential elements of a user-centered design methodology.

Chapter 7

Methodology

➤ A methodological standard describes how to do user-centered design—select a good methodology that will work for your organization.

➤ You probably already have a system development life cycle in place, but it is probably not a user-centered methodology. You may need to retrofit a user-centered process onto or in front of the current technical methodology.

➤ Implement a quick test of your life cycle. Is it user-centered? Take the test in this chapter.

➤ Review The Schaffer Method as an example of a proven user-centered process.

Some people do not like standard development methodologies. They prefer to work with each project and figure out what is needed for that one project without thinking of standard practices. They may feel that this is a creative process, but it is also inefficient and non-repeatable.

Having a user-centered design process or methodology in place means that the critical steps to make a product usable will not be missed. It also means that all projects will follow a similar method and thereby ensure a standard level of quality.

A methodological standard primarily plays the role of a memory jogger. It makes sure that you do not forget to do some of the hundreds of major steps needed for good design. Implementing a methodology also provides your company with a mature process, a systematic methodology that can be organized, supported with tools, monitored, and improved. A standard process of user-centered design is essential, and the methodology you choose or develop must enable you to be reliable, successful, and efficient in your design process.

This chapter describes how to choose a methodology and outlines some of the challenges you may experience as you integrate it into your current development process.

What to Look for in a User-Centered Methodology

Mature development organizations today use a defined system development life cycle for software development. This means they have a plan for how to develop software that includes an entire cycle from feasibility through programming and implementation. Some of these are industry standards with software tools available, such as the Rational Unified Process (RUP), and others are proprietary processes developed within companies. Although some software development life cycles may mention usability, they do not include a comprehensive set of steps necessary in order to follow a user-centered design process. Software development life cycle methodologies concentrate on the technical aspects of building a software product, as they should. They do not make the engineering of the user experience and tasks the primary focus of the development. This means they build applications from the technology and data, inside out. User-centered design is a different way to approach development because it concentrates on the user and the user tasks, rather than on technical and programming issues. Following a user-centered design process is the only way to reliably create practical, useful, usable, and satisfying technology products. In a user-centered process, you will design the user experience first, then let that drive the technology as shown in Figure 7-1.

Almost all practitioners in the field agree on the steps required to follow a user-centered design process. You can document these steps yourself and build your own user-centered design process. Accomplishing this may, however, be slow, expensive, and time-consuming. You should undertake this task only if you have senior usability staff with many years of experience in order to ensure you are following industry best practices. In most cases, you are far better off buying a process and then customizing it for your organization.

Your user-centered process affects the way that functional specifications are created. For example, you will craft the user taskflows before you worry too much about the database structures. The user-centered process will mostly bolt onto the front of your technology process. Then throughout the software development process, steps connect the user-centered process to the work that the technical staff is doing and the documents created to go to the programming staff. There are then lots of linkages to create to ensure that the methods stay coordinated, and document handoffs need to be identified at a detailed level.

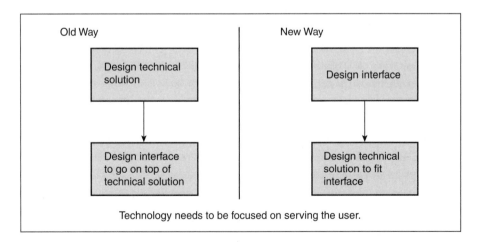

Figure 7-1: *The "Old" Technical-Centered Solution Needs to Be Replaced by the "New" User-Centered Solution.*

This is not to say that technical limitations are ignored in the early design phases. Interface designers need to know about the technical issues for a particular project. They need to understand what the technology can and cannot do in order to ensure that they have used the technology to the fullest and yet have not designed something technically difficult to implement. However, the primary concern is meeting the customer needs. You need to engineer the user experience and performance and derive the user interface structure to support this user taskflow. Then the technical staff can design the software to support the user interface design. This might lead to pulling together data from a dozen servers to provide a summary view when entering the site, using graphic preloads to shorten the download time on a Web site, or using cookies to see that users get book offers that relate to their needs. The technology has a huge role to play, but it needs to be focused on the needs of the users.

Select a user-centered methodology that meets the following criteria.

- *It must be comprehensive.* It is not acceptable to have a process that relies on usability testing alone—it must address the whole life cycle.
- *It must be user-centered.* This means it must be firmly grounded in designing for an optimal user experience and performance first, and the interface design and technology must be based on the user needs. It must take user needs into account and must actually access representative users for data supporting the design and feedback.
- *It must have a complete set of activities defined and deliverable documents required.* It should be not a loose collection of ideas but a specific set of activities with actual documentation throughout the process.
- *It must fit with corporate realities.* Ill-defined or changing business objects are by far the biggest cause of feature creep. The user-centered design process needs to include steps that bring together the diverse strategic views and ideas of your organization's stakeholders. There need to be activities in the process to ensure that all key stakeholders contribute and feel heard.

Integrating Usability into the Development Cycle

By Janice Nall, Chief, Communication Technologies Branch, National Cancer Institute

We really want usability to be so integrated into the development cycle that it's just like graphics: It's just a process, and it's where you insert it into the process that matters. It's not at the end—when it's ready to go out the door—it's at the very beginning. We just want to make usability mainstream and not constantly have to argue the cause. We are still in that mode; we feel like we have to prove ourselves every day.

If we can get it into the next realm where we can take it to the next step, where we are not spending all the time justifying why we need to do it, we can pursue research to get answers to the questions that don't have answers. I think there is a huge interest in really pushing the science—from our end certainly, but from across the federal government also. We must make better-informed decisions and start advancing the field, sharing that knowledge and really disseminating what all of us are learning effectively.

- *It must be a good fit for your organization's size and criticality of work.* Large organizations that build large and critical applications should have a more thorough process and more detailed documentation.

- *It should be supported.* While it may be wonderful to have a process described in a book, implementation requires much more. It requires training, templates, tools, and a set of support services. It is daunting if you have to create them all or cobble them together from a diverse set of sources. You might find a pretty good user-centered design methodology—you might get it from the Web or from a friend. But then the issue becomes what is required to support that methodology. Expect to spend a good half year of work if you have to create all the deliverable document formats, questionnaires, tools, and standards. Expect to spend another half year to develop training to support the standard.

- *It must be able to work with your current development life cycle.* This is no small task and is discussed later in this chapter.

- *It should ensure that the methodology has a cross-cultural localization process* where the design is evaluated for language and culture issues (only if you are doing cross-cultural or international development).

An Outline of The Schaffer Method

To give a sense of what a user-centered methodology should include, this section outlines The Schaffer Method, a methodology based on the practices that have evolved at HFI over the last 20 years. Driven by cycles of data gathering and refinement, this method pulls in the knowledge and vision of the organization and harmonizes them with user needs and limitations. This solid process for ensuring quality design includes designing screens by using templates (instead of "reinventing the wheel" each time) and supports deployment and localization to different cultures. We follow this process consistently at HFI and have integrated it in practice with almost every commercial system development process and hundreds of home-brew methods.

Figure 7-2 shows an overview of the methodology. The first column lists the planning phases, and the second column lists working phases and deliverable documents. To the right are the cycles of data gathering and major design iterations plus the estimated time frames. The following subsections describe the HFI process for implementing this user-centered methodology.

The Plan Evaluation and Structure Phase

This is the project organization phase, during which you identify the main activities and allocate adequate staff and time. You also establish the extent of usability work required.

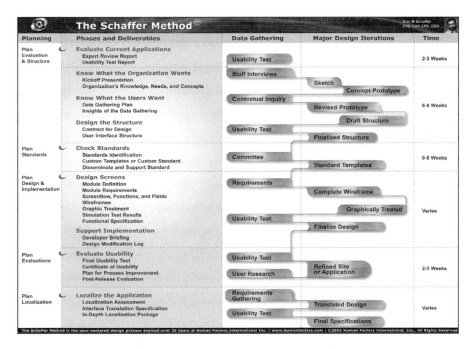

Figure 7-2: *The Schaffer Method*[1]

Up to five planning cycles are recommended during the entire process of a full development life cycle. In following this recommendation, it is unlikely that the resource estimates for any phase will be inaccurate. If you try to plan for the entire development at once, you are guessing how long it will take to create the design without knowing what you are creating.

The first cycle happens before the project begins. It provides a solid plan for the user interface structure and a rough estimate of subsequent work. Until the user interface structure is defined, you really do not know what is being built or how many screens will be covered in the functional specifications, so making estimates beyond the structure is quite challenging.

Your planning efforts include the following:

- Project plan
- Standards plan

---

1. For a larger version, please see the Appendix.

- Functional specifications plan
- Usability evaluation plan
- Localization/cross-cultural plan

Evaluate Current Applications

In this first step, you evaluate any existing applications and identify potential improvements. If the planned design is a revision of an existing application, you need to review and usability test the existing design. Reviewing the existing design helps you identify areas that need special emphasis during redesign, and conducting usability tests clearly illustrates the impact of usability problems on the business. This usability test is valuable for convincing stakeholders of the importance of usability issues in the design.

Know What the Organization Wants

After you have evaluated your current application, you need to identify the business strategy and the direction your organization would like to take before beginning work on the actual design. A good project clearly identifies the needs and strategies of the organization and makes them fit with the end user's capabilities, limitations, and aspirations.

An important source of organizational information is the wealth of data most organizations accumulate over time. Marketing studies, click stream reports, and strategic analyses are all excellent sources of data.

Talking to key stakeholders and internal staff is also an essential way to gather organizational information. Start by learning what the executive leaders want in the new application. Understand their vision as it impacts the users. What is the unique value? Why is it worthwhile? Why is it better than competitive alternatives? What has been the history for past applications?

Based on the information collected, make a very rough sketch of the design that reflects the organization's overall ideas for the future interface. The stakeholders may want to begin coding this vision, but this is ill advised. First, you need to find out what the users want.

Know What the Users Want

You need to understand the different users and their needs before you can design a solid user interface structure. Knowing the user is critical because a successful design facilitates what the user wants. There are many ways to learn about users, but the best method is to conduct in-depth interviews with representative users. Through this, you can learn the user characteristics—psychographics as opposed to demographics. It is important to know what users care about, their skills, and their deep mental models of the application's tasks. In-depth interviews also help you understand the users' physical and social environments. At the end of this phase, don't document everything; record only the key insights that really matter to the design.

Design the Structure

Once you know what users want and need, you can begin the design process. Our years of experience at HFI have shown that 80% of usability is determined by a good interface structure: It ensures that users can understand what is offered, find things quickly, and navigate efficiently.

Begin by creating a simple **task design**—a flowchart of the future user experience. Fine-tune and expand it to create the contract for design, which can be used as a solid foundation for user interface design once all the stakeholders have reached a consensus. The contract for design simply lists the personas for the typical intended users and then describes the expected scenarios for each. The stakeholders all sign off on it. This means that stakeholders are less likely to suddenly surface a whole new type of user or needed task later in the design process. It therefore provides a firm foundation for on-going work.

With this agreement in place, design the navigational structure of the user interface. If the project is critical, develop two or three alternative or parallel designs to generate extra insights into the best navigation method, and create a set of possible graphic treatments. Finally, conduct a user test to improve and validate the navigation structure and graphic look.

The result is a user interface structure. This structure is the most critical part of the design and includes the concept, metaphor, function set, information architecture, navigational mechanism, and stylistic appearance. If the structure is poorly designed, there is no way to fix it with good wording, layout, control selection, color, or graphics.

The Plan Standards Phase

The second phase addresses the preparation of a template-based standard (as covered in Chapter 9 on interface design standards). This activity is not needed if a standard already exists. If a new standard is needed, start 6–8 weeks before you need to use the standard and you will avoid a project delay due to the need for standards creation.

Check Standards

Some people do not like the idea of standards because they feel their creativity is being limited. But most developers now appreciate interface standards that provide definite direction and decrease the likelihood of needing to make many changes later. Standards are effective: They save time, improve design quality, provide consistency, and allow creativity to be focused on things that matter.

Identify all the standards that apply to the design. These may include branding, style guides, industry standards, and legal requirements. There must be a template-based standard to make ongoing design efficient and consistent. **Templates** (or patterns) are screen design examples that incorporate all the standard's decisions. They define page types and provide an actual screen example that can be followed as a best practice model. If necessary, customize the standards for the application or—even better—for use throughout the whole company. These templates become the DNA for the screen designs, so it makes sense to perfect them in every way possible. They need to reflect not only the standards requirements but also must reflect good design principles (wording, layout, color selection, graphic usage, control selection, and so on).

The Plan Design and Implementation Phase

The next planning phase covers the development of functional specifications. It is very difficult to estimate the time requirements of this phase until the application is fully defined. It is not possible to come up with a time estimate by simply multiplying the estimate for one screen by the total number of screens—some screens take a couple of hours to create, while others take weeks. Your estimate will also be highly dependent on the quality of design staff available. However, it is possible to accurately plan support for the implementation process at this time.

Design Screens

Screen designs are created once the navigation is designed and the standard templates are in place. Normally, designing all the content pages is a labor-intensive task, but with a solid navigational structure in place and templates to work with, the design of each individual screen takes less time.

The usability practitioners create a functional specification at the end of this process. The **functional specification** describes each screen or page and its contents, provides a picture, and describes the interactions and actions the user can take. This is the end of the intensive usability work on the project. The application can now be designed; the remaining challenges typically involve technical implementation.

During this phase, the screens are designed as well as tested and iterated.

Support Implementation

After the usability practitioners finalize the functional specification, they hand it over to the implementation team—the programming staff members who will develop the product. This is also the time when a process may be instituted to place content in the design.

The usability team members need to constantly communicate with the developers as the developers work to implement the functional specification. If the developers have not been intimately involved in the usability engineering process, take time to brief them. It is important that they understand the background and intent so they appreciate the criticality of the design decisions. Communicate with them on an ongoing basis to review, negotiate, and log changes made to the specification because of implementation issues. Ensure that the user experience is not negatively impacted by these changes.

This is also the phase when you arrange to feed content into the design. This may require the support of **content developers**—staff who develop and manage the actual text, illustrations, and other content in the product. It is also important to provide standards, training, and coaching. Anyone who is developing content or creating actual screens and coding them needs to understand the standards and templates and how to use them.

The Plan Evaluations Phase

The fourth phase identifies the processes and resources for post-release evaluations. **Post-release evaluations** are somewhat similar to the first cycle of usability testing and are *summative* tests—they test whether the design works, as opposed to *formative* testing that refines the design. During previous phases, there should be a complete program of review and refinement. However, in the final testing, the new design is measured to see whether it met the human experience and performance objectives of the new site or application.

This final evaluation is not the same as quality assurance testing. **Quality assurance testing** is part of the software development process and ensures that the product is functioning correctly from a technical point of view. The final evaluation phase of a user-centered design process ensures that the product is usable, not that it is functional.

Usability testing is done throughout the design process, but in most cases, a more formal simulation test is conducted at the end to measure success and identify the few remaining problems. It is important to formulate action plans for solving problems identified by this final testing and to document all accepted action plans and their

A.G. Edwards' Usability Process and Methodology

By Pat Malecek, AVP, CUA,
User Experience Manager, A.G. Edwards & Sons, Inc.

I've heard from usability practitioners at other companies that it's fairly common to have a formal and well-documented methodology in place but that it's not often followed to the letter. We certainly have a very well-documented methodology—whether or not it's followed to the letter varies from project to project, depending on scope, schedule, and things of that nature.

We have a summary version of that methodology that we are putting the finishing touches on. It is a Product Development Life Cycle that we've crafted, and it provides a much simpler view. This life-cycle document was developed by both the business and technical sides, and it puts forth a mutually agreeable methodology that calls for early attention to presentation issues and lots of opportunity for iteration and look-and-feel corrections. We are hoping to disseminate the life-cycle document through all the relevant parties because it shows in simple terms where various usability issues could be addressed.

In terms of examples of the usability practices that we put into the process—in the grandest terms, we do it all. We've completed projects in which we go out and interview users, and we do card sorting, and then we go to navigation mock-ups and move through paper mock-ups and test paper mock-ups, all the way through to a finished product. And when things are being done with great urgency, typically we do wireframing, and when I say "we," it's our user experience designers. So they have the proper skills and the proper knowledge, and then they'll take those mock-ups—if time doesn't permit to test with the appropriate users groups—at the very least, they will take those mock-ups to a cluster of people and do some informal testing to shake out some of the big bugs.

progress. Upon completion of the final usability testing, consider having a certified usability professional approve each deliverable in your project.

Once the application is in service, it makes sense to gather additional data to identify enhancements and ensure that the design objectives were actually met. Also, the development process requires regular improvement, so it can be helpful to hold a postmortem meeting to discuss this project, document the lessons learned, and identify areas that could be improved.

The Plan Localization Phase

This final phase is necessary to ensure success in cases where the application will be localized for additional geographies and cultures. This may require translation to other languages and will most certainly require the consideration of cultural differences. Such differences include major issues regarding work styles, practical issues of environments and resources, and detailed challenges of different field formats and conventions.

A Quick Check of Your Methodology

You may discover that your current methodology has some user-centered design in it, but you might be wondering if it is a good process. The following exercise helps you test it. HFI developed this test based on feedback from 35 usability professionals with a great deal of cumulative experience in the field. They were asked what the most important activities in user-centered design are. HFI then asked the participants to provide weightings for how much the activities impacted the quality of the results and fine-tuned the rating system by working with clients. This quick check works for Web sites, applications, and any other software designs.

To take the test, look at the 15 design activities described in Table 7-1 on pages 112–113. Check which ones are included in your methodology, then add up the points to get your Usability Quotient. The maximum rating is 100. If your methodology has less than 75 or so, it is probably in need of enhancement. If it is below 50, you probably need a whole new process.

The Challenges of Retrofitting a Development Life Cycle

It is a rare company that does not have an existing system development life cycle. Your company may have purchased a method, or perhaps you built one from scratch. In either case, it is unusual to find that the method already provides a user-centered methodology. Perhaps someday every method will follow the user-centered paradigm, but as of today it is likely that the existing methodology is not user-centered.

Occasionally, a company needs a whole new development process. This scenario occurs not just within brand-new organizations—a new development process may also be needed when there is a major change in the technology or scope, such as the switch from simple Web brochures to complex Web application development. Usually, however, the organization already has a software development process and needs to deal with the relationship between the existing process and the newer user-centered design methodology. The methods have to be interwoven with proper communication and handoffs between the different types of development staff.

There are three likely situations if there is an existing process: classic methodologies that are not user-centered, patches where some user-centered activities have been added, and classic methods that just have usability testing added. These same situations tend to appear in commercial methodologies that do not have an ideal user-centered process. The following subsections explore these three scenarios in greater detail.

Table 7-1: *HFI's Usability Quotient Checklist*

	Checklist Items	Explanation	Notes	UQ Value (if Complete)
1.	Define brand, style, and tone	Define the character of the site with a list of adjectives (e. g., cool, high tech, trendy; stable, reliable, simple).	Use existing brand values where appropriate.	4
2.	Define user population	Describe the users in terms of skills, knowledge, interests, objectives, and concerns.	Also known as user profiles or personae, this addresses user's psychographics instead of simple demographics.	8
3.	Set usability objectives	List of specific objectives from the user's viewpoint (e.g., complete a trade faster than the competitor, or rate the site easier to use than driving to store to buy the product).	Usability objectives, goals, or criteria can be based on task time and error performance or satisfaction survey ratings.	7
4.	Define user environment	Describe the user's environment (e.g., interruptions?), pattern of work (e.g., uses once a month), and social context (e.g., needs to get supervisor's approval).	Base the description on interviews and observations made during a contextual inquiry.	6
5.	Analyze current tasks	Understand how the site functions are done today. Draw a taskflow diagram.	Use contextual inquiry techniques. Develop user scenarios of use which can be derived from use cases.	9
6.	Redesign tasks	Develop a story of how the functions and tasks will be done in the new application. Describe the scenarios and make them simple and easy. Optimize use of new technology.	Reengineer and match the taskflow to the limitations of the technology used in the application under development.	13
7.	Verify useful with unique value	Check that the site will offer substantial benefits, beyond other sites, applications, or manual facilities.	Does the site offer compelling value to make users return? Is it sticky?	4

	Checklist Items	Explanation	Notes	UQ Value (if Complete)
8. ❑	Verify practical	Conduct a formal walkthrough of the taskflow design to ensure that it will be practical in the real-world environment.	Is the site practical from a commonsense point of view?	3
9. ❑	Test navigation	Run a short usability test to make sure people can find things on the prototyped main navigation pages.	Use low-fidelity paper or similar prototypes.	9
10. ❑	Test aesthetic appeal	Run the test that validates the positive appeal of the visual design. Also check that the design supports the branding objectives.	Use the test of brand perception to measure that the design is aesthetically pleasing and supports the brand.	2
11. ❑	Use page design standards	Design most pages by copying from sample templates.	Use generic or customized best practice page templates.	7
12. ❑	Complete detailed design by staff with training in usability	Get at least basic training in usability before designing pages.	Can be an HFI-Certified Usability Analyst.	8
13. ❑	Review all pages systematically for usability and consistency	Review the pages for usability and consistency. Do this with someone who is *not* on the development team.	Do a walkthrough of the site using the most important user tasks and user profiles.	7
14. ❑	Usability test site or application	Perform a simulation test where users complete a set of tasks and see where they have problems. Fix the major problems.	Use in-person, one-on-one testing with the "think aloud" protocol. Can be supplemented with remote online testing.	7
15. ❑	Monitor initial usage	Review initial usage with click stream analysis and user data. Fix significant problems.	Establish success metrics and monitor them.	6
			Project's Usability Quotient (0–100).	❑

Using Classic Methodologies

Most software development methodologies seem to follow a classic process. One such method is the waterfall method, in which the steps follow logically and build in sequence. Another type is the spiraling method, where design cycles are more iterative. Occasionally, there is some sort of rapid method, which moves quickly to prototyping and tends to work well only for small projects. From my viewpoint, all of these are classic methods because they fail to put the user first: These methods identify business and technical functions and database design and middleware in progress, before the user tasks and actions are identified and taken into account. Therefore, when I call these *classic* I mean *old* but not in any way *good*.

Retrofitting a Method That Has Added User-Centered Activities

A second situation occurs where there has already been an attempt to add user-centered activities to a software methodology. The problem is that the attempt is always well intentioned but is often not well done. Instead of a thorough user-centered design process, you have a software methodology process with a few usability activities added here and there. The effort is neither thorough nor sustained.

Both software methodologies and user-centered design methodologies have lots of steps. For each, the steps are important, and they need to be done in a certain order. However, the steps are different. Trying to retrofit the steps of one onto the steps of the other does not work. Trying to force the tools, templates, or documentation of one to fit the other also does not work.

Retrofitting a Development Process That Has Only Usability Testing

The third and last situation is when a team has created a user-centered methodology by simply adding usability testing to its software development process. This is a common practice, though very ineffective. It is like being reprimanded for reaching the wrong destination when you were given no maps, compass, or navigation tools for the journey.

Without a full user-centered process, performing a usability test at the end of the development process just highlights the unacceptable nature of the design. This kind of result can be sad and frustrating. There is usually little that can be done other than to go ahead and release the poor design.

But with a user-centered process, the usability test becomes a source of useful and easily implemented changes. These changes are not radical because the structural design has been solidly built and tested long ago. So, there is no need to throw out the structural design. The insights tend to be small in the form of minor changes to wording, layout, and graphic treatment, and they tend to be easily implemented. Yet this type of final usability testing is well worth doing.

Implementing this type of user-centered process can be compared to creating a wooden statue. In the early phases, there is sawing. Then you will need to use a chisel. Finally, there is sandpaper. The final usability testing becomes the fine sandpaper. Without the full process in place, it is just like trying to create a wooden statue by starting with fine sandpaper.

Following a user-centered design methodology makes your design activities reliable and repeatable. Without a methodology, it is difficult to produce high-quality designs. The maturity of your methodology is a reflection of your organization's commitment to user-centered design, so be sure to invest in the most effective methodology available. The next chapter outlines some of the tools, templates, and testing facilities that are instrumental to implementing your methodology.

Chapter 8

Tools, Templates, and Testing Facilities

> If you throw usability staff into the organization without the right equipment, they are going to seem slow, inefficient, and impractical.

> Get tools (e.g., lab equipment), templates (e.g., reusable questionnaires), and testing facilities. These items form an essential toolkit—the core infrastructure for routine usability work.

> Your toolkit makes it efficient to complete the methodology. To determine the toolkit you need, review your methodology.

A well-trained staff in a room with nothing but paper can outdesign a poorly trained staff equipped with a state-of-the-art facility.

The main value of facilities, tools, and templates is time savings. Instead of creating a testing form from scratch every time a test is needed, a usability engineer can take an existing form and modify it for a client's specific test in about 20 minutes. Creating the concept for a test and the forms from scratch takes days or even weeks. So, hire good staff members, and supply them with the tools that make a difference. This chapter outlines the tools you need, the templates that are helpful, and usability testing facilities that will help your staff be most efficient and effective.

Note, however, that by the time this book is published, some of the tools and templates described here may be outdated because new developments happen all the time. For example, you may hear that usability testing labs have recently moved from being "marginally useful in special circumstances" to becoming a practical part of almost every test. Or you may learn that remote testing, which isn't used often today, is becoming far more practical and therefore much more widely used. **Remote testing** is usability testing performed at a distance; the participant and the facilitator will not be in the room together (in fact, may not be on the same continent), yet the facilitator can still monitor what the participant is doing and saying. Because toolsets will likely change, a skeptical attitude about these tools is useful—if a tool does not really make a difference in the design, spend your money another way.

Introduction to Your Toolkit

Your methodology points to the facilities, tools, and templates you need. For example, if the methodology specifies that a test of branding occurs at a certain point, you will want to have templates for reusable questionnaires and a standard template for the final report.

If you update your methodology, you may need to update the corresponding tools, templates, and facilities. Also, new facilities, tools, and templates might lead you to change your methodology. For example, online prototyping has become easier, so you might move it further up into the design cycle. Or, as remote testing becomes more feasible and useful, you may add it to your methodology and develop new tools and templates to fit it. However, be careful about implementing these kinds of changes because some "amazing" breakthroughs are actually not that useful.

The following sections cover the infrastructure you should consider implementing at your company. They also explore scenarios and priorities for each facility.

Testing Facilities

Depending on circumstances, testing facilities can range from a simple office setting or a hotel room to a full-blown usability testing lab. You do not have to have a full usability testing lab in order to conduct usability testing. If office space is at a premium, the office of one of the usability team members can be used for testing. There may not be a one-way mirror, special equipment, or videotaping. There may be only a few chairs, a desk, and a computer. However, skilled staff members can still successfully create and run the tests. Similarly, it is quite acceptable to use a conference room to run tests; however, it is critical that the room be reasonably quiet and free of visual and auditory interruptions. For this reason, it is best never to use participants' workspaces for testing. You can observe them there, but workspaces are not good places to run tests.

There are a number of reasons for having a formal and dedicated usability testing facility. One reason is that designating a space for testing shows a commitment to testing within the organization. It is nice to have a room or perhaps a suite with that label, but this will not have value so much in supporting the work as in making a political statement. Of course, the facility becomes an albatross if it is not regularly used. Unfortunately, some labs left unused later become storage spaces.

There is a real value to having a quality testing environment. While the results of running tests in storage closets can still be quite good, it is best to have a testing environment that makes the participants and the facilitator feel comfortable and important. If you can make the test a relaxed experience, you will get more accurate and complete results. At the same time, facilities that feel imposing and overly scientific should be avoided—you do not want the evaluation environment to feel too formal. That's why usability engineers usually call people *participants* instead of *subjects*; no one likes to feel like a lab rat!

Facilitating a test is a very demanding activity. It takes focus, and it's difficult, if not impossible, for one person to keep the test process running, observe the nuances of the results, and record data. There is no additional energy or time left to greet participants, provide the initial forms, and give them compensation once the testing is complete. Therefore, it is very useful to have additional staff available to handle these functions. Professional testing facilities have support staff.

In some cases, you will need a facility that is geographically separated from your offices. You might decide to do testing in a number of cities intermittently, or you might even need to complete testing in these different cities quite often. In this scenario, it makes sense to have a relationship with a testing facility in each location. These testing facilities are generally set up for marketing studies, but they work well for usability testing. It is also possible to use a conference room in a hotel, but the testing facilities provide such valuable amenities as a greeter, a one-way mirror, built-in sound and video, and usually a more comfortable atmosphere.

Whether you obtain a contract with a professional testing facility or choose to build your own testing space, there are a few advantages associated with obtaining a professional testing facility versus using a simple conference room. Figures 8-1 and 8-2 show the appearance of a typical professional testing facility. Your facility may have a one-way mirror. Most people can tell when you have a one-way mirror, so if your facility has one in place, you should be straightforward about it. With a proper briefing, the mirror works very well. Developers, business owners, and marketing and usability staff can come and observe without disturbing the test. They can discuss what they see and send in their questions to the test facilitator. In place of a one-way mirror you can also use video feeds to adjacent rooms to allow others to observe without disturbing the test.

Figure 8-1: *Observer's Side of a Professional Testing Facility Using a One-Way Mirror* (see Plate 1)[1]

Figure 8-2: *User's Side of a Professional Testing Facility Using a One-Way Mirror* (see Plate 2)[2]

---

1. Photo courtesy of The Bureau of Labor Statistics
2. Photo courtesy of The Bureau of Labor Statistics

Recording of Testing Sessions

There is some value to recording the data gathering and testing sessions. Professional facilities have video capability, and the new portable labs allow video as part of their software.

There are two types of tape usage. One common practice is to provide a full videotape of the session for the record. A continuous tape is made of the test, and you end up with many hours of tape. However, if someone says, "I don't believe the user actually did that," you can offer to let him or her see the appropriate portion of the tape. In other cases, a much shorter highlights tape is culled from the full videotaping sessions. This edited video, 5–10 minutes long, shows key findings of the usability testing through the voices and actions of the participants themselves. Carefully selected examples on well-edited highlights tapes often can depoliticize the usability test findings: It is no longer the "opinion" of the tester; it is the voice of the participant. Highlights tapes effectively grip the audience's attention when used as part of the final presentation. This is a very effective practice. There is nothing like showing video of the users in action.

In the past, recording sessions were prohibitively expensive, but with the new "shoebox" usability equipment available today (see Figure 8-3), the cost is much more reasonable. This shoebox equipment includes a TV camera, microphone, monitor, and a remote marker to make it easy to find interesting tape segments. There is in fact no tape, just a high-capacity hard drive to save the data, so it is also far easier to edit and present the results. This ease of use, combined with its reasonable cost, makes the shoebox lab a practical alternative to traditional equipment.

Most labs are moving to digital means of recording to make video editing easier as well. Using this new technology, you can put parts of the video record in the report (see the sample of a test presentation video in Figure 8-4). The lab software lets you record the user's facial expressions and the activity on the screen.

A few labs use a special type of equipment called an eye-tracking device. It lets you track where the user's eye is fixating. You can gain

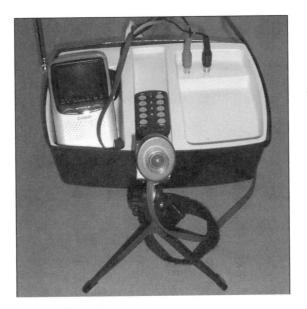

Figure 8-3: *Shoebox Usability Equipment*

Figure 8-4: *Example of a Video Record from a Usability Test (see Plate 3)*

a lot of information from this device. You can see users scanning around the page because they are lost or scanning an image because they cannot tell if it is selectable.

Eye-tracking devices are very useful for research purposes. For example, studies have shown that people start scanning in the main area of a Web page and initially ignore the logo, tabs, and left-hand navigation [Schroeder 1998] and that people's eyes are drawn first to areas that have saturated colors (pure bright colors), darker areas, and areas of visual complexity [Najjar 1990].

You do not need an eye-tracking device in order to run an excellent usability test. A good facilitator can see where the user is looking anyway and can supply you with very similar data. An eye-tracking device is expensive and requires setup time, so you probably won't use it for routine usability tests. It may come in handy, however, in a remote usability test since the facilitator will not be physically present with the participant.

Modeling Tools and Software

Most of the important usability work can be completed with a simple office suite. It may help to have a flowcharting package, and you also need software for graphics work, but that's about all the software you need. You also need to be able to use a word processor to document meetings and descriptions, and you need a tool to mock up screens and pages. Which tool you use is not as critical as making sure that the usability staff members are comfortable with the tool and that they do not get distracted or waste time writing "code" to make the screen mock-ups work. Some people prefer a graphics program like Adobe Photoshop, but a presentation tool like Microsoft PowerPoint works just as well. Some usability staff are already facile in a tool such as Microsoft Visio. Whatever tool your staff members already know how to use that allows them to quickly mock up screens and pages is the best tool to use.

Sophisticated modeling tools may or may not be necessary. Available software can assist in the development of very large taskflows and the modeling of taskflow behavior. An example of this type of software is Micro Saint (a product made by Micro Analysis and Design, Inc.), which supports task modeling. I have seen this software used to good effect in very complex and critical applications, especially in the military design arena. However, I have yet to see this software used to make a difference to commercial Web sites or applications.

Limited modeling tools are available for usability work. You may wish to create your own. At our company, we built an application called the Task Modeler. It is basically a specialized spreadsheet that helps add up the number of clicks, mouse movements, and keystrokes used to complete a task. Using this application on a group of tasks representative of the work to be completed on a given interface provides a good indication of the time it will take an expert user to use the software. This data is important because when measuring the speed of task completion during a usability test, you're measuring only how fast users are during their initial usage, not how fast they would be after extended experience with the interface. During the test, users spend only minutes with the software, so they will not be experts on using the interface. Yet there are many cases when you are designing for expert users. Also, you don't want to make the classic blunder of designing for first usage only. For example, a menu design that can be used easily and quickly by novices is a much better alternative to using commands initially, but you may then find the commands are faster once learned. If the software will be used full time, going with the menu can be a million-dollar mistake. In this case, we built our own tool.

Many companies have purchased tools to track Web sites and provide feedback and statistics on usage. Some of these tools claim to provide usability information and are useful for performing quick checks and validation. For example, there are tools that let you know if your alt text tags are missing (accessibility tools) or if you are using too long a line length. Be wary, however, of tools that track download times for a page, or how many users clicked on a page, or how much time people spent on a Web page, independent of other information. While this information can be useful to know, it can also be misleading. Why did a user spend only 3 seconds on a page? Was it because (a) the page is poorly designed, (b) the page is well de-signed and the user got what he or she wanted right away, or (c) the page *before* was poorly designed, so the user clicked on the wrong link? You cannot tell any of this just by reading a report on where people went and how long they stayed. Nothing can replace a trained usability professional evaluating a screen or page or watch-ing and interpreting users performing a task.

Data Gathering and Testing Techniques

Usability data gathering and testing are some of the most valuable tasks your usability team can do. While the phrase "run a usability test" is a general term, keep in mind that there is not a single type of usability test—there are many different types. For example, there are tests of branding, early paper prototyping tests for conceptual design, and later tests on robust working prototypes. You must select the type of test needed for where you are in your develop-ment process and then create the correct type of test questionnaires to support the testing.

You can save a lot of money and time by having an initial set of questions and then customizing them as needed for each test. Hav-ing a list of standard tests helps to quickly plan the testing, but each test needs its own set of forms, such as video consent forms, facilita-tor scripts, task instructions, and so on. Defining and creating pre-designed templates can save countless hours. While no template for a given type of test works for all situations, there is certainly value in having a template as part of your infrastructure. Some example template forms include those listed below.

- The **screener** is an essential questionnaire used to select partici-pants for a study. The screener can help eliminate participants who are too sophisticated or too inexperienced. In some cases, a template can be developed and used repeatedly for each study that will access those types of users, though typically the tem-plate must be modified for each test.

- **Usability testing routine forms** are a family of forms you need when running usability tests. They are not very exciting, but they are quite necessary. For example, you must have an informed consent form to get the participant's agreement to participate. Without this form in place, you are in violation of ethics in human research and can be sued. You may also need demographics forms and forms to acknowledge compensation.

As mentioned, there is more than one type of usability test. Below are descriptions of different tests. Which one you use depends on what questions you are trying to answer.

- **Brand perception tests** let you see how the user perceives the current Web site or application. One version of this test is for a single design, and a variant of the test can also be run as a comparison with competitors' designs. Another version of this type of test involves the selection of the best among suggested designs. This test can be conducted with designs from different graphic artists or even different agencies. Regardless of the scenario, the questionnaire for this test must be customized to reflect the company's target brand values. You need to pick the brand values you are interested in testing. What brand values are you looking for, and which do you want to make sure to avoid? Trendy, warm, friendly, sophisticated, "tech-y" ... you need to customize the questionnaire to get at the data you are interested in.

- If you ask users if they want a given function, they almost always say yes. If you give them a list of potential functions and ask them to rate how important they are, they rate most as very important. But if you give them a list of possible functions and say they can have only three, you get interesting results. This test, called a **functional salience test**, is a great way to identify the relative importance of functions.

- A **test of affordance** determines whether users can tell what they can select on a page. You simply give users a printed copy of a page and tell them, "Circle the items you think you can select and click on." You will see if there are selectable items that users cannot tell are selectable. You will also see if there are items that are not selectable that make users think they *can* select them.

- **"Think aloud" tests** consist of a whole family of tests where the user is told to do a series of tasks, which are observed. Users are asked to read out loud as they work and tell the facilitator what they are thinking. This is a great way to find problems in a design. You can also estimate how long it will take users to complete tasks.

- The **card sort test** is a useful method if you are trying to find how users categorize the topics in a Web site or application. You create stacks of cards with one item on each card, and then the participants group the cards in a way that makes sense to them. Software can help collect and analyze the groupings used by different participants. The software uses cluster analysis and gives results that can guide the information structure of the design.[3]

- While the card sort test can help guide the design, you can use the **reverse card sort method** to check whether the design worked. You give the participants a list of items and see if they can figure out where to go to find them. If they can find them, the navigational structure is self-evident.

- **Subjective ratings** are a large family of tests that allow users to describe how they feel about your site or application. They decompose or break down the perceptions to allow you to more easily track the cause of problems. For example, you might find that people love the colors but feel that the site is very slow. These findings need to be carefully considered. You might find lots of users saying they want a search facility, but this may actually indicate that there is a problem with the structure of the site. The stated desire for a search facility is often just a symptom of being lost in a poor navigational structure.

The Special Needs of International Testing

International testing is far harder to coordinate than just arranging for facilities and participants in lots of countries and racking up lots of air miles. Test procedures don't work cross-culturally; therefore, international testing takes special capabilities and infrastructure. You need to deal with translation issues and adjust the testing

---

3. IBM's EZSort programs are an example of cluster analysis software. For more information, visit www3.ibm.com/ibm/easy/eou_ext.nsf/Publish/410.

methodology based on cultural differences. For example, in some cultures it is not polite to criticize, so the usual methods of asking users to think aloud and expecting that they will say what they think is wrong with the product may not work. If you are testing internationally, make sure you leave enough time to deal with these different circumstances.

The Bollywood Method[4]

By Apala Lahiri Chavan, Managing Director,
Human Factors International, Mumbai, India

The main challenge with usability testing in Asia is that it is impolite to tell someone they have a bad design. It is embarrassing within this culture to admit that you cannot find something, so it is very hard to get feedback.

I conducted a test on a site that offered airline tickets for sale. I used a conventional simulation testing method and got little feedback. I could see that users were not succeeding, but they would not willingly discuss the problems they were experiencing.

I then tried a new method I had developed, called the Bollywood Method. Bollywood is the Hollywood of India and makes far more movies each year than Hollywood does. Bollywood movies are famous for having long and emotionally involved plots. The movies have great pathos and excitement. In applying the Bollywood Method to this testing scenario, I described a dire fantasy situation. I asked each participant to imagine that his or her beautiful, young, and innocent niece is about to be married. But suddenly the family receives news that the prospective groom is a member of the underground. He is a hit man! His whole life story is a sham, *and he is already married!* The participant has sole possession of this evidence and must book airline tickets to Bangalore for him- or herself and the groom's current wife. Time is of the essence!

(continued)

---

4. Based on Chavan [2002].

The Bollywood Method (cont.)

The test participants willingly entered this fantasy, and with great excitement they began the ticket booking process. Even minor difficulties they encountered resulted in immediate and incisive commentary. The participants complained about the button naming and placement. They pointed out the number of extra steps in booking. The fantasy situation gave them license to communicate in a way they never would have under normal evaluation methods.

This method worked well in India and may even be able to be generalized to special situations in North America and other places where participants may hesitate to communicate freely.

Recruiting Interview and Testing Participants

Usability tests typically require fewer participants than marketing research studies because the findings in usability tests are usually qualitative, rather than statistically descriptive. In usability testing, you are not trying to generalize your results and estimate the numbers or percentage of people who feel or would react to a product in a certain way. You are exploring. You are trying to determine whether there are usability issues, what they are if they do exist, and how you might solve them. This means you are trying to delve into the psychology of your users. And this requires that the participants you test are representative of the target population of actual users. You are going to need to find representative users for data gathering and usability testing.

In-house users, while easy to find, aren't usually acceptable participants because they probably care more about the company than the real users do. They see the application as being worthy of additional effort and might exaggerate its value, or they might not flag aspects of the design that make it impractical. They are also familiar with the company's in-house language, concepts, attitude, and mindset, and they might even have different aesthetic values and perceptions than typical end users.

In one case it is fine to perform tests with in-house users: If you are actually building an application for the internal staff members, it is appropriate to sample them. This is usually a very easy and informal process; the staff members just need to be screened and scheduled.

Lots of market research and usability testing companies have staffs of screeners—clerical-level staff who call lists of potential partici-pants and follow the questions in a special questionnaire (also called a screener, as noted earlier in the chapter). The staff members use the questionnaire to select participants who fit the criteria for the study. Participants are typically offered a fee of $100 to $200 each, depend-ing on how stringent the required match criteria are. Some of these facilities have databases of potential participants. This can be conve-nient, but the lists may be overused. (Some people seem to be mak-ing a part-time job out of participating in studies!) You may want a fresher list. To accomplish this, you may need to ask the recruiting firm about the people in their databases. You can shop around for databases and recruiters, and you can specify that the participants must not have been in any studies during the last 12 months. This may make your recruiting more expensive because it may be harder to find participants. If you need general participants, for example, people between the ages of 20 and 60 who purchase goods from the Web at least once every 3 months, it may be relatively easy to find "fresh" participants. If you need people who work in a copy center who have never used a particular type of software, you will pay more for this type of recruiting. It is good to have relationships already set up with companies that can help you recruit participants.

If your user group is current customers, it may be possible to develop a list of customers and have the staff screeners work from that list. This may be easier and more cost-effective than using a recruiting firm. In some cases, you can have internal staff work tem-porarily as screeners. This costs very little unless you need to hire in-house staff to work as screeners full time. Using in-house screen-ers saves money over hiring a screener consulting firm, but the in-house screeners will need to be trained. Usability consultants are already trained and just charge you per project. But having a smooth machine for obtaining study participants helps keep usability work progressing—problems with obtaining participants is the single most common source for the delay of usability projects.

A whole series of deliverable documents result from proper usability work. It is true that some people approach usability without much of a concept of deliverables. They think they can just study the user and good things will happen. That may be true—good things *may* happen. But to make usability work efficient and repeatable requires an organized set of deliverable documents. The deliverables give a clear focus and a set of milestones for usability work. As an example, Table 8-1 lists the major deliverables in The Schaffer Method.

Table 8-1: *The Major Deliverables in The Schaffer Method*

Schaffer Method Deliverables	
Expert Review Report	Wireframes
Usability Test Report	Graphic Treatment
Kickoff Presentation	Simulation Test Results
Data Gathering Plan	Functional Specification
Insight of the Data Gathering	Developer Briefing
Contract for Design	Design Modification Log
User Interface Structure	Final Usability Test
Standards Identification	Plan for Process Improvement
Custom Standard	Post Release Evaluation
Module Definition	Localization Assessment
Module Requirements	Interface Translation Specification
Screen Flow, Functions, and Fields	

It takes time to create good deliverables, but they offer several benefits.

- They document that steps in the methodology are actually completed.
- They allow work to be communicated to others, for instance, key stakeholders and development staff.
- They allow work and processes to be repeated.

Most deliverables require several smaller deliverables to create the end product. So, in the end, there are hundreds of deliverables. Imagine that you needed to create these deliverables from scratch for each project, figuring out the appropriate document structure and inventing the style of presentation. The level of investment for this would make usability engineering programs prohibitive in cost and time. If each of the 23 deliverables listed in Table 8-1 took just ½ a day to create structurally, then you would add 11½ days to the project.

If usability is to be routine, standard reusable deliverables are indispensable. They help organize the project and save valuable time. Standard deliverables also make it is easier for managers to check a project's progress because they know the full set of deliverables to expect. Finally, using standard deliverables also makes it easier to get oriented and to review an unfamiliar project.

The value of the tools, templates, and facilities outlined in this chapter is that they save you valuable time. However, it remains critical to pick the items most appropriate for your efforts. It is not sensible to invest in something just because it is a new technology. Refer back to your strategy often, and remember to let your methodology determine your toolkit. The next chapter provides information on another valuable time-saver—the implementation of interface design standards.

Chapter 9

Interface Design Standards

➤ If you look at any application or environment, you can identify a few screen types that account for about 85% of all screen development. Templates are representations of these key screen types and can be used as the "DNA" on which the entire application is built.

➤ In addition to templates, a design standard should include general presentation and operation rules.

➤ Interface design standards save development time, maintain consistency in designs, improve usability, and make maintenance easier.

➤ There are a number of ways to create a design standard. Developing one from scratch should be a last resort.

➤ Design standards can be applied to a Web site and also to all of an organization's public sites, extranets, and intranet.

➤ Don't develop standards unless you have a clear plan and resources for disseminating, supporting, and enforcing the standards. The completion of the standards is the beginning of the real process.

When teaching classes on design standards, I always start by asking how many people are excited by the prospect of doing all their future design work under a strict set of standards. Few people respond with enthusiasm. Many feel that design standards will be a terrible restriction, and implementing a standard feels like eliminating creativity. In reality, standards (both methodological and design) are like the well-known melodies in jazz (which musicians also call "standards"). Jazz standards provide a baseline melody, which the artist uses as a starting place from which to begin tasteful improvisation. Interface design standards are essential to provide a similar starting place and format. But it takes a great artist to work within the standard and make something worthwhile, just as it takes a great musician to work within the standards in jazz and create something special.

This chapter explains what interface standards are, explores why they help a usability team be efficient, and describes the content and characteristics of effective standards.

What Is an Interface Design Standard?

As you create a usability engineering infrastructure, there is probably no more critical component than *interface design standards*. Done right, these standards help users visiting your page feel like they have worked on a page like it before. With standards, the development is faster and maintenance is easier. But these design standards are *not* methodological standards, *not* software coding standards, *not* style guides, and *not* design principle documents.

Methodological standards, such as those described in Chapter 7 on user-centered design methodology, describe the process for design but do not specify the precise design conventions.

Software design standards apply to the design of the underlying software. They do not address the presentation-layer design conventions at all.

Style guides are usually like the style guides for writing a manuscript—they document specific fonts, colors, and the proper use of images and may even state the tone for the text. They may make suggestions on other topics, but they do not ensure full design consistency. These types of guidelines are useful, but they are different than design standards. Basically, a style guide documents rules for presentation style. But the style guide does not get to a level of specificity necessary to give the user the experience of real operational consistency. The style guide does not dictate the navigational and operational details of each screen, nor does it indicate what button is used to go forward. We need rules down to the level of selecting OK, Enter, or Continue for the button names.

Organizations often want to document **design principles**. The hope is that the document will tell designers how to do good interface design. Design principles do not address the specifics needed to ensure design consistency. Also, people rarely read such documents. It is usually better to spend money on training rather than on writing such a document.

Interface design standards set very specific requirements for the way that screens look and operate. The key to these standards is the idea of a reusable screen type, pattern, or screen design template.

Screen Design Templates

If you look at any given Web environment, you will find a limited number of page types that account for about 85% of the development.[1] Some of the most common page types are home pages, forms, wizards, and database maintenance pages. The number of page types is not infinite; you might need a total of 10–15 page types for an entire environment.

Make templates of commonly used page types and then modify them to create the specific instances you need. For example, on a form you would change the headers and field labels. But you would not need to change the Enter button name or the conventions of left alignment and required field marking.

---

1. This figure is based on HFI's 20 years of experience in user interface design and standards development.

The templates you create will become the foundation of your template-based standards; these standards can be developed for computer software screens as well as Web pages. Figure 9-1 shows an example of a template for a wizard. This template example reflects good design practices, even for the parts of the interface design that are not standard, and will be customized by the developers when using this particular wizard.

A template should include accompanying documentation on when to use a page type, rules for the parts of the page that are standardized, a prototyping tool (which lets the template be turned into an individual page or screen quickly), and reusable code.

Instead of creating each page from scratch, the developer can consider the user's task and then select the template page or pages that support that taskflow. This means that instead of having to work at

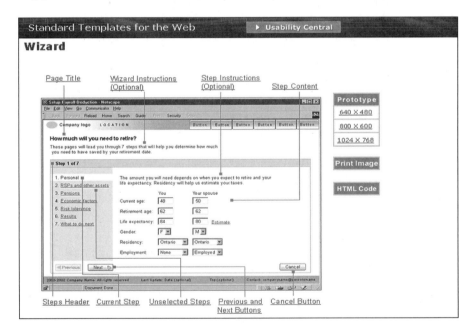

Figure 9-1: *Example of a Reusable Standard Page Template for a Wizard, Taken from Usability Central Gold* [2]

2. Usability Central Gold is a product from HFI that contains a complete set of standard page templates for most Web site designs.

Plate 1: *Observer's Side of a Professional*
Testing Facility Using a One-Way Mirror (see Figure 8-1)

Plate 2: *User's Side of a Professional Testing Facility Using a One-Way Mirror* (see Figure 8-2)

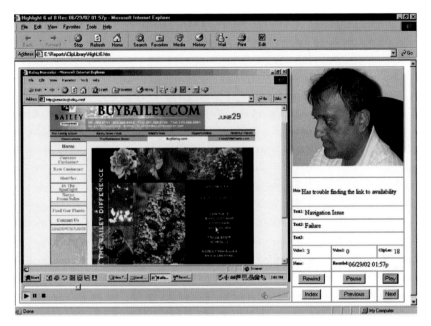

Plate 3: *Example of a Video Record from a Usability Test*
(see Figure 8-4)

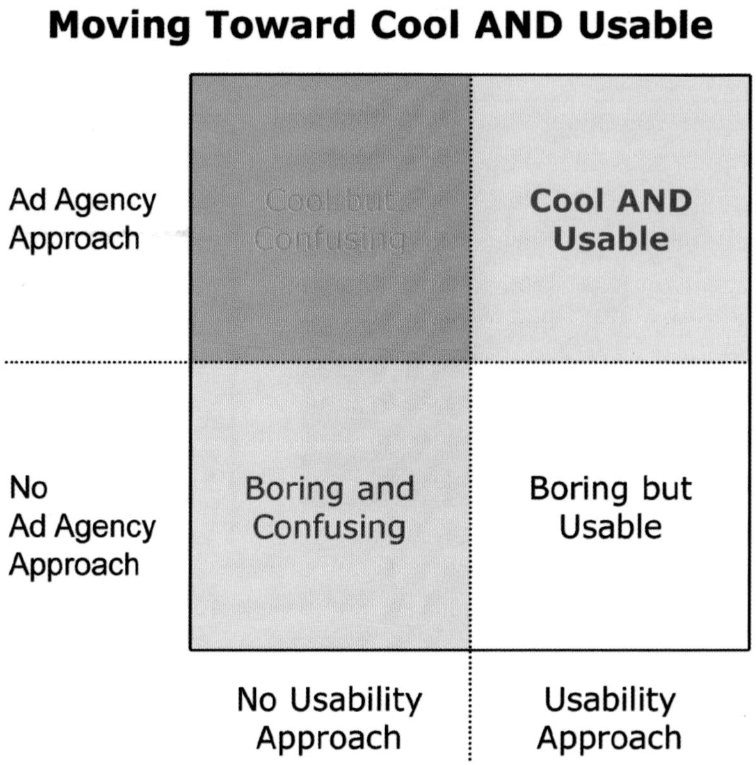

Moving Toward Cool AND Usable

	No Usability Approach	Usability Approach
Ad Agency Approach	Cool but Confusing	**Cool AND Usable**
No Ad Agency Approach	Boring and Confusing	Boring but Usable

Plate 4: *Dr. John Sorflaten's Matrix of Usability and Creativity* (see Figure 12-1)

a very detailed level and generate pages from scratch, the developer can work at a higher level. He or she can identify the type of page needed and then choose the best template. The developer can decide whether to use a menu, a display table, or a wizard and then view the example of each necessary page type and copy the conventions. If necessary, developers can create hybrid pages combining multiple page types. Without the design standard, developers invest time creating everything, from a name for each button to navigational features. The names and features they select are often ergonomically poor, and the user is left to try to figure out the meaning of the buttons on each page. This is why a design standard needs to be specific in these types of details.

The templates are the "DNA" for all designs, so they must provide an example of quality design in all respects. However, you need to identify and document the aspects of the template that are actually standards. Standards fall into two categories: basic standards and optional standards. The **basic standards** are things that you must have if you are going to use a given page type. They include the features that will identify the page type for the user and the universal ways of operating the screen.

The optional standards are a little more complex, but you need to have this concept in place to make the standards work. The **optional standards** are things that may or may not be needed. For example, on a search page, you may or may not require a link for an advanced search. The optional standard says that if you don't need an advanced search, you can leave it out. If you do need it, then you *must* call it "Advanced Search" and place it in a consistent spot on the page. These rules generally need to be documented so that developers can look up these items and know what is actually required.

Improvements in technology for applying reusable code and content management have made the template concept work even better. These technologies make it easy to use program modules to support a given function on multiple pages. Once there is a defined page type, it is easy for developers to write code to support it. This means that designers actually need to do *more* work if they want to violate the standard—they have to go into the reusable module and edit it.

Other Contents of a Design Standard

While page templates are the core of a good design standard, other sections and materials are needed too. Some requirements and issues, such as those listed below, go across all the page types:

- Header and footer designs
- Error handling (pop-ups, inline error messages, embedded messages, and graphic treatments and formats for message wording)
- Button labels (guidelines such as "Use Next to get the following page" and "Do not use Forward, Continue, →, OK, Up, or Down")
- Justification of text
- Alignment of labels and data fields
- Formats for data (such as addresses, phone numbers, and so on)
- Fonts
- Restrictions on color usage

Not that there isn't some overlap between style guide issues and design standards. In many cases, the entire contents of the style guide can be incorporated into the general principles section of the design standard.

The Scope of Design Standards

It is important to note what is *not* included in the design standard. Except where there is a need to create a unified style and theme, it is best to leave significant design freedom to the developers. For example, within an intranet there may be hundreds of sites, and many will require different themes. The design standard should generally address only the elements critical to the user's recognition and the operation of each page type. However, there are cases where more restrictions are needed to ensure a consistent brand perception.

It is important not to mix the design rationale and research behind various decisions within the design standard; this would create an unmanageable amount of work and a vast body of information. Such documentation can overwhelm developers and other users of the design standards. The design standard should describe just the *results* of all this research. Books and training provide information on the actual research and rationale.

Some design standards document the windowing environment or the browser operation; however, it is a waste of time to document things you will buy and cannot change. These environments and operations are described enough in the documentation from the vendor. This includes purchased facilities, like e-mail clients, along with anything you will build only once. For example, standards for the design of a staff directory aren't necessary because these standards apply only to that one application, and it is a one-time deliverable. So it is far better to just develop specifications and build the directory, instead of writing a standard that will guide the specification.

Another pitfall in this standardization process is the specification of underlying technology and coding practices. There is no question that technical standards are needed, but the design standards specify requirements for the presentation layer. These requirements must be carefully reviewed to ensure that they can be implemented. But there is no reason to make the presentation-layer standards dependent on the technology. It is wise to code the presentation layer separately. It is also wise to make standards for middleware, databases, and coding practices that are separate from the design standards.

An interface design standard can cover a single application, a suite of applications, a single Web site, or a family of Web sites. For example, a financial institution might have a site for retail banking, a site for commercial banking, a brokerage site, and a corporate site. These sites might have different headers and footers. Different style guides might dictate different colors. But at the end of a form, all the sites use the *same word* to say Enter. They do not call the same function by different names (e.g., Enter, Submit, OK, Continue, Go). A single standard can cover a whole family of sites. This means that customers going from one site to another see a company that is consistent in its practices.

It is also possible to have a single design standard cover public Web sites, extranets, and the intranet. This is a bit more of a stretch. Some activities provided in the intranet could never be offered to the public. For example, the standard for an intranet or extranet site may need page types that would not be used on the Internet, such as a page type for complex database maintenance. This type of page will be efficient for trained or computer-savvy users, but it will be a disaster if offered to the general public. The database maintenance page is not needed for the public Web site, and therefore the public site developers simply avoid using it.

However, if you can, there is a big advantage to using the same interface design conventions between public Web, extranet, and intranet sites. It is increasingly common for a single function or module of content to be displayed in multiple environments. For example, the public must see the current product features—and marketing staff, customer service representatives, and suppliers must view the same features too. Therefore, if the design standards are consistent, that page can be shared with all users.

You can also develop standards that go across different operating systems. The controls for the form might look a bit different in shape and style for the different operating systems, but most of the conventions can be generalized successfully. While the differences in hardware platforms force some differences in page designs, you must make sure that a user who accidentally follows the wrong platform convention has no serious problems. For example, if you make the Enter key mean "take an action" in one environment and "move to the next field" in another, you will frustrate users and create significant mistakes.

Design standards can cover a very wide range of different applications, but the one place where they cannot usually stretch is between platforms and technologies. For example, a standard for a voice response system cannot be applied to Web design. The standard scripting that works for telephone interactions does not apply to the Web. Also, as of this writing, it is difficult to develop a standard for both windowing applications and Web sites because the user expectations are quite different for each one. Therefore, you need separate standards, though they should be as consistent and compatible as possible (e.g., the page design and operation should be as similar as possible).

The Value of Design Standards

Design standards save development time. For example, instead of developers spending hours reinventing design decisions, like whether to call a button Enter or OK and where to place this button, they can just refer to the design standards. This also ensures that a team of developers follows the same guidelines and makes the application or Web pages consistent.

A design standard also saves development time by supporting the creation of reusable code. For example, if you define a single way for a search and list page to work, you can create reusable code to support that design. The application of that page type then simply requires making changes to the base code. This also reduces the need for quality assurance because the reusable code has already been debugged.

Design standards make applications more usable: Because the designs are consistent, users can generalize their knowledge of how one screen works to all the other screens of the same type. If the standard is successful, the users look at the screen and think, "Hey! I've seen screens like this before." Then the screen works the way they expect. This has tremendous value, even if the designs are a bit suboptimal or idiosyncratic. In fact, the standard designs are likely to be far superior to the ad hoc designs ergonomically. The ad hoc designs are created by an individual with limited experience and limited time. The standard collects the best thinking of an entire committee (generally including highly experienced usability staff). The decisions of the committee are leveraged across hundreds of designs. Therefore, the committee feels justified in working harder on each design decision.

Design standards make maintenance and upgrades easier too. For example, the development of a new DHTML slider control might make some graphic display standards obsolete. Assume that this change is so wonderful that all designs really have to be changed to take advantage of this new control. This requires that the standard be upgraded and the change be applied to the designs across the organization. This is a lot of work. However, think of how much easier it will be because of the standard! Without a standard, you must scan through a wilderness of different graphic display designs, consider each one separately, reinvent each design, code it, and then test it. With a standard, you can review the page types and find the places where the slider is needed. These changes can then be systematically rippled across all those page types.

A couple of intangible advantages of standards are quite significant. The attention and creativity of developers shift: Instead of having to worry about how to reinvent another type of menu, they can focus on how to implement the design. They can be creative in understanding the user taskflows and making improvements; instead of renaming the OK button, they can find a faster way to process claims.

Another intangible value is the creation of a unified brand—a critical element in a public Web site or a private intranet site. The standard can give a site a sense of cohesion, organization, and reliability. Many customers become confused when they find that designs are different between modules of a single application or sections of a Web site. The standard design needs to be crafted to support the brand. The consistent designs create a positive impression and can support the specific characteristics desired.

While developers may initially resist the use of a design standard, if you are doing a significant amount of development, the standard will be worthwhile. It is actually more common now for more experienced developers to welcome usable standards. They want someone to help them with the design of the pages or screens so that users can successfully run the applications.

The Process and Cost of Developing Standards

Standards development should be a high priority when creating a strategy and should be placed early in the activities list. There are three ways to get a design standard: You can buy a generic standard, customize a generic standard, or create a standard from scratch.

If you have a small company or a lean operation with typical interface needs, it makes sense to start with a purchased standard. Clearly, such a standard will be generic and you'll eventually need to add existing conventions, special branding, specific user needs, and so on, but it will give your company a head start. You can start small, with customizations, and gradually build on.

If you have a large company or your environment has many special needs, you need a full design standard. A full standard should include a customized set of page types, the specific designs to reflect your conventions and user needs, your brand (not just in color and logo), and the personality of your company, down to the style of interaction and page layout.

Purchased standards are a good starting point for a custom standard. It is quicker to modify a standard than to create one from scratch. Full customization of a generic standard generally takes six to eight weeks.

In some situations you will need to create a standard from scratch. The most typical case is one where you have an environment that is so idiosyncratic you can find no generic standard that remotely fits your requirements. An example of this is a new interface technology that, as yet, has no generic standards available. Another example is a corporate culture that strongly values internally designed materials. If you decide to create design standards from scratch, be aware that this can be a long, painful process with lots of challenges. It will take a minimum of three months and perhaps even up to a year to do it right. The process would typically require $180,000 for a consultant's support.

If you are customizing a standard or creating one from scratch, you probably need a committee-driven process with a usability consultant as a facilitator. This method starts with a review of your strategy, business areas, applications, and sites to determine the types of screens you need. Then the consultant designs a good example of each page type (these may be based partly on your screens and partly on a purchased standard). This set of designs goes into a committee process. The committee is made up of the key opinion leaders in the development organizations. The committee reviews the designs and decides whether or not the approach for each screen type is appropriate. This is a concrete process; the committee is basically asked, "Is this the way you want to do a menu/form/wizard?" The final standard is based on their decisions. The process for customizing a generic standard takes about six to eight weeks and costs about $100,000 (for the modification of the standards deliverable, as well as a consultant to guide you). However, if you can make your own design decisions without so much facilitation and high-level guidance, the cost can be cut nearly in half.

No matter which method you use, here is one important piece of advice: Ensure that the standards effort will not be running out of steam by the time the standard is written. Sometimes committees suffer from endless cycles of iteration during the standards creation process. After a year-long process, the standard may finally be complete, but the committee members may by now be so sick of the standards process that there is no motivation to push the standard into actual usage. Remember that the completion of the standards is the beginning of the real process, so it is important to pace yourself accordingly. No matter which method you choose to create a standard, be sure that you have the energy, will, and resources to follow through.

Disseminating, Supporting, and Enforcing Standards

Before investing in a standard, be sure to plan for its dissemination and support. This means training, consulting, and enforcement. One idea is to phase it in, as mentioned in Chapter 5. Even though the design standard will really support creativity and improve an application's or Web site's usability, the feelings against standards are real. Therefore, if you do not work to spread and support the standard, nothing will happen. Your investment in developing the standard will be lost. In fact, you should not develop standards unless there is a clear plan and budget for dissemination and support. Getting the standards written is just the beginning of the process.

At HFI, we have had a significant controversy over the years regarding whether a paper or an online standards document is better. A paper document is easier to work with in some ways; the developer is already using the full screen for design work, so an online standard requires switching between windows. However, there is a significant cost in having a paper version—it must be printed and distributed. Updates will be required, and then it will be hard to tell if you have the current version. Also, increasingly, the standard comes with online materials like reusable code.

If you have an online version, everyone has access, and when it's updated, everyone gets the new version at the same time. Of course, this is very different than everyone actually using the standard. You have to get the word out. It is good to send notices of various kinds and to highlight a link to the standard on the developer's intranet pages. But these efforts alone will not be enough to ensure appropriate use of the standard.

It is essential to provide training on the standard. Standards training is different than training on general usability engineering methods. This training needs to sell developers on the value of a standard. It needs to convince them that the standard will not stifle their creativity and that it will actually make them more creative, effective, and professional. With standards, there is still plenty of room for creativity, but the quality and consistency of standards make for better designs.

The standards training also needs to show people how to use the design standards. This means understanding the structure of the design standards themselves and how to find things within them. Developers must be familiar with the different types of pages and be able to pick the ones that fit a given situation. They must also know how to use the general presentation rules. All this material can usually be presented in a half-day class. Done well, these classes increase acceptance of the standards and also convey the information people need to operate effectively within the standards.

Preparing reusable code is a powerful way to support the standards. Often, a single standard is implemented in different environments, and these need to be considered. For example, your menu may be created in Macromedia Dreamweaver, Microsoft FrontPage, and by old-fashioned HTML coders working in Microsoft Notepad. This is fine. The standard dictates what the user sees, and thereby interface consistency is maintained across these environments. But it makes sense to select the main environment(s) and create reusable code as a specific project. This may mean creating a template for each page type in a browser environment. This makes the development process faster and means that developers have to work harder to violate the standard. It also means that maintenance is easier because there is common code underlying the various pages. Alternatively, the page designs may be placed in a content management tool. Whatever the environment, the introduction of reusable code helps move the standard into general usage.

With dissemination of the standard, along with training and tools that provide support, developers will start to try to follow the standard. They will sometimes get stuck or have misconceptions. They might think that the content in the examples must be copied into the designs or that optional standards are required, or they might not understand which page to use for a given user task. Therefore, designate one person or team as a resource to contact for help. The best way to support this need is usually with internal consultants. Internal consultants are key staff members within the central usability organization (see Chapter 14) that can answer typical questions quickly. Implementing this type of program saves a huge amount of time. The internal consultants can also help developers quickly resolve design questions and ensure that they apply the standards correctly. If developers have trouble working with the standards and cannot get help, the results will be poor, and the entire standardization effort might be scuttled.

If a developer is not sure which page to use, the internal consultants can help. But if a developer reinvents a page, there is no question for the internal consultants to answer. The developer is completely happy, but the standard is undermined. There is no feedback to the developer and no immediate feedback to management. There is only a silent unraveling of your standards investment and, eventually, poor usability of the application itself. The only answer to this type of scenario is some type of enforcement.

Enforcement of standards is a hot topic. It is a frightening idea and often feels awful, but some form of enforcement is required. The trick is to make it fit the corporate culture. In some cultures, heavy-handed enforcement is natural and normal. In other environments, the idea of enforcement is abhorrent. In this type of culture, don't call it enforcement, but at least institute feedback. Have the designs reviewed by a usability engineer, and point out to the developers specific places where they have violated the standards. The most common and worrisome problem is that developers might reinvent page types. They may attempt to create a new type of menu, for example. This review cycle is the time to point to the standard menu and suggest that the developers could use an approved page type to fit their needs. In some cases, all you can do is give feedback. In other environments, you might require changes and report the level of compliance to the developer's manager. The standards dissemination and support require the most effort during the short term. In time, developers will refer to the design standards and follow the conventions they have learned.

Even after you have developed the standards, they will still need some attention. The standard is a living document. You will need to make improvements, add page types, and insert clarifications in areas where you get frequent consulting questions. It is also likely that areas where refinements are needed will be brought to your attention after your showcase project. This refinement will lead to further improvements and greater buy-in from all users.

Implementing interface design standards should be a high priority for any serious user-centered design strategy. The initial investment for creating standards may seem high, but following template-based options can easily pay back this cost. The return on investment in regard to branding, consistency, navigation, performance, and time savings far outweighs any initial cost. Remember, the completion of the standards is the beginning of the real process—using them. The next chapter outlines the steps for achieving a successful showcase project, which will also provide an opportunity to refine your organization's standards.

Chapter 10

Showcase Projects

➤ A showcase project is the "test flight" of the new usability engineering infrastructure.

➤ Your showcase project offers an opportunity to refine the methodology and toolkit. It can give new staff practical experience and can demonstrate the feasibility and value of usability work in your actual business environment.

➤ Use very senior staff members to lead the showcase. Also, select the right project based on size, criticality, timing, performance, and visibility.

➤ Put extra effort into the showcase. It must both refine the process and demonstrate good usability engineering. A showcase project is challenging, groundbreaking work.

A test pilot proves the plane's performance and uncovers the bugs as he or she tests a new design for the first time. The design works well on paper, and the systems should work because highly trained professionals built each one. Yet it is almost certain that something will go wrong. The systems must integrate and operate in a variety of environments.

A showcase project is a high profile interface design project to which you apply your usability best practices. Showcase projects are similar to these test flights: For the first time, you are bringing together a new skill set, methodology, facilities, templates, tools, and standards, and it may be the first time you are doing user-centered design. It is also a real project—it has the goals of a real project (like making money), but it also provides a "shakeout" of the usability process and infrastructure. The results of the showcase create the impetus for the true incorporation of user-centered design into the organization. Like a test flight, you can be pretty sure something will fail to work out the way you planned it, and it will take some serious skill to avoid a crash.

The showcase project must be a success because this is your first opportunity to demonstrate the value of the process. The quality of the staff on a usability project is the most critical determinant of project success. So put your best usability resources on the showcase, and give them the most competent and supportive development staff.

Your usability team will handle the showcase, preferably with help from an outside expert. Problems are likely to occur, and it is important to manage them with grace. The showcase team must complete the project using the unproven infrastructure and, at the end of the project, demonstrate how effective and valuable the usability work has been.

This chapter describes the importance of a showcase project, discusses how to select the right team and project for the showcase, outlines some of the other factors you need to consider, and provides some tips on running a successful showcase.

The Value of a Showcase Project

The Setup phase of institutionalization integrates a user-centered methodology with the existing development process and plans the handoffs and communication requirements. Setup requires the creation of a training program, deliverable document templates, tools, and standards. The showcase project is the culmination of this phase. No matter how much diligent work has been completed, this plan is likely to encounter some problems because this is the first time the usability plans, procedures, deliverables, methodology, and infrastructure are being used on a large critical project. The usability team is likely to find problems and deficits, so the showcase becomes a chance to refine the products of the Setup phase and demonstrate the ability of the usability team to work together with the development team.

The value of a showcase project is demonstrating that user-centered design is possible in the development environment and that usability engineering has a real business impact. More developers now have experience with user-centered design, but there often seems to be skepticism that usability engineering can work in "this" organization. Developers may suspect that management will not let it work. The showcase project is an opportunity for the management team to demonstrate that they support the user-centered process and rely on systematic and scientific design.

Gaining Acceptance for the Usability Team
By Arnie Lund, Director of Design and Usability, Microsoft

Microsoft has a rich history of design and usability that spans the last 15 years. During that time, people have been messaging the right things about user experience and the process of institutionalizing design, and usability is well on its way. It is still true, however, that often you will hear people stand up in front of a room and introduce *usability* as "These are the people who make things easy to use" and introduce *design* as "These are the people who make things look cool." We want to be introduced—both design and usability—as "These are the people who deliver value for the user and make money for Microsoft." We want to be viewed as a critical core competency, positioned at the heart of the development process, as opposed to being viewed as a nice add-on to development.

(continued)

Gaining Acceptance for the Usability Team (cont.)

Our challenge in figuring out how to position ourselves is to avoid battles over territory. It is really about how to articulate our role in a way that works with the process that Microsoft has evolved to make sure that software can be cranked out effectively, quickly, and systematically. We've got to find our place in that world.

The advice I've given people is to start with a great foundation and deliver first-class work. On my team, our focus is on making sure that our product teams are getting what they need from us, that users are satisfied, and that the product teams understand user input is important to product success.

The advice I give to managers is to realize that you can't stop at doing the job well. As a discipline we have a tendency to focus on what we're doing, on the technical issues, and on what makes something a usable, great design. We feel that we're not really politicians and we're not really diplomats. We just prefer to do what we do. Because what we do doesn't necessarily have a lot of cultural stickiness, however, managers have to continually sell the importance of what we do and educate people on what we need to be effective.

I think a better model for usability and design in organizations is being a company within the company. You've got to have a great product, but you also have to continually market your product, and you have to explore how to expand your market. You also need to come up with new products building from your core competency.

The showcase project can demonstrate the feasibility and value of usability work in the actual business environment. By applying usability methods to an important project and producing a successful, usable product on time and within budget, you can quickly make the case for user-centered design in your organization.

Another important value of the showcase project is the refinement of the design standards. Standard templates hold up to actual design problems very well. Yet it is common to find some changes required in the first use of the standards. Therefore, the showcase project becomes an opportunity to refine the standards. You might discover new required page types, some necessary refinements to a given page design, corrections to the error handling processes or field formats, or needed clarifications to the wording of the standards. It makes sense to plan a new release of the standards after the showcase design is complete.

Once the project is finished, be sure to capture all the potential benefits from the project, update the methodology and design standards if needed, and pull together lessons learned. Most importantly, document and share the business impact of the work. The usability team should perform these wrap-up responsibilities.

You will want to have metrics that assess the value of the project. Before/after metrics capture the variables that matter most to the business. But numbers alone fail to tell the real story; being able to see what was done and a concrete example of how the design was changed means even more.

Selecting the Right Staff and Project

The most critical success factor in making the showcase work is the quality and experience of the staff. Selecting the right staff members for the project is the most important step. The second most critical factor is the actual project chosen for the showcase. When looking for a good showcase project, consider its type, size, duration, usability value, and visibility.

Although work on future projects will be routine and will be performed by staff members with a variety of expertise and years of experience, the showcase project is the first project and should therefore have the most senior and experienced people assigned to it.

The Right Staff

The leader of usability work for the showcase project needs to be a highly skilled veteran. Just as you would not hire a newbie as a test pilot, you would not pick a usability lead with only a few weeks of training and little experience. At a minimum, I would look for someone with a decade of usability engineering experience—someone who is technically savvy and flexible. I also suggest choosing someone who can communicate well. He or she needs to be a good troubleshooter too—the project lead must find creative solutions so the project moves forward and the process can be refined. Finally, the project lead must be a good salesperson within the showcase process. It is helpful to have the ability to directly bring out the developers' feelings and doubts and sell the developers on the value of user-centered design.

The showcase project is also a potential venue for learning. With a very senior leader in place, it is possible to have some assistants with less experience help with the project and learn about the process. However, you should make this opportunity a second priority. There is enough to manage on most showcase projects without employing too many inexperienced helpers. Let most training happen on subsequent projects, once the process is refined and proven.

The executive champion is an invaluable resource during the showcase project. Political roadblocks are most likely to occur during the showcase project, so this is a critical time for the executive champion to be available to help remove obstacles. For example, the marketing staff might be reluctant to allow direct contact with customers, or an executive might have trouble letting go of his or her personal role in making design decisions. The executive champion must be alert to these roadblocks.

The Right Project

There are two types of projects you can choose as the showcase project: (1) the development of a new site or application from scratch and (2) the revision of an existing facility. Each choice has advantages and disadvantages. A revision scenario is usually best because it allows for a visual and numeric contrast between the existing facility and the new design. If you are building a showcase project from scratch, you can show how the design evolved and how valuable insights were incorporated. But with this type of project, you don't get the stark contrast with a baseline design that had little usability engineering attention.

It is important not to pick a project that is too large. In the classic project-planning book, *The Mythical Man-Month*, Frederick Brooks [1995] gives a graphic description of how things change as they get bigger. He cites the example of a NASA hanger that has problems beyond those of normal-sized buildings. The hanger is big enough to develop its own internal weather; it rains inside the building. He then describes how huge projects have a unique level of management and coordination problems. The showcase project is in a tough enough position without struggling with problems related to size.

While it is bad practice to have a huge showcase project, it is also inadvisable to choose a project that is very small. Small projects fail to exercise the process and may also make some of the methodology and documentation involved seem trivial and unimportant. Small projects can let problems slip through. For example, a small project may make it appear that simplistic rapid prototyping will work well, but this method will not work on sizable projects. The project must exercise the entire process and ensure that facilities are in place for coordination and completion of systematic design. A project with fewer than five developers is likely to be too small for a showcase project.

The optimal showcase project should have five to fifteen technical developers. But a mitigating factor is the size of projects typically completed by your organization. If you usually do very small or large projects, choosing a more typical project makes sense.

While it may be tempting to choose a critical project that must get usability help urgently, this kind of project is actually a poor candidate for a showcase project. If it needs help immediately, it is likely to be too large, already in progress, or a political nightmare. These are not good attributes for a showcase project. From a political and business viewpoint, you may need and want to apply usability techniques on this project—but try to avoid making that project your showcase. Create a special team to manage that project. Staff it and manage it as if it were a special project that had to be completed well. But keep it aside and don't make it count as a showcase project; you don't want to slow down the process or pose any possible risk to your institutionalization program with a poorly selected showcase.

Additional factors such as the time line, user impact, and visibility may also be important considerations. These are described below.

Consider the Time Line

There are a number of factors to consider regarding the time line of the project. As discussed above, it's best to use a project that is just starting. While it is possible to join an ongoing project and retrofit the user-centered process, this is a complicating factor. Using an ongoing process can make it seem that usability work is slowing the design and can create pressure on the team to work too quickly in a "catch-up" mode. If the team has worked through some conceptual designs and even created some initial design sketches, it is feasible to convert these into a showcase. But if the project already has detailed designs with many screens designed and specified, it is too late.

The project duration is also an important consideration when selecting a showcase. Very short projects are rarely big enough to demonstrate the whole process. Very long projects do demonstrate the whole process, but they are completed long after the results of the showcase are needed to propel the institutionalization effort forward. The ideal showcase project would last four to eight months. This time frame is measured from the start of the project to a point where results are given to the developers for implementation. This may be the point at which prototype testing is complete and definitively successful, or it may be the point when real customers are online. But the main concern should be maintaining momentum for the usability institutionalization effort. If the showcase is stalled in a long development cycle, your institutionalization effort will most likely stall too.

Consider the Impact on Users

When selecting a showcase project, ensure that there can be a substantial value to the usability effort. That is, a project is a much less likely candidate for a showcase if it has few end users. Consider an internal project for customer service representatives (CSRs). Let's say you can conservatively save 20% of the call-handling time by doing good usability work. With a call support group of 1,000 staff members (with an annual burdened cost of $70,000 per person), the value of that savings is $14 million per year. This makes a very nice showcase example. It is motivating for the team and makes a great story for the final presentations.

Now consider a call support group with just 6 people. You can expend the same effort on this project and get the same 20% improvement in call performance time. The resulting savings would be $84,000. This amount will probably not pay for the showcase project. In fact, the question will rightly come up that little can be done with the one-fifth of a CSR's time that is saved. It may be hard to reassign one-fifth of a CSR, and the actual labor saved might be worth only about $70,000. So, look for a project that has more end users than this example.

Showcase projects are better if the user experience or performance is very important. For example, with 911 call-handling software involving police dispatch, lives are at stake, and a significant improvement makes a compelling story. In the same way, foreign exchange traders can make millions of dollars by being a few milliseconds faster with a deal. In e-commerce, an unhappy user is less likely to buy and less likely to return to the site. Give the showcase team a major contribution to make, based on usability.

Consider Visibility

Projects that many people interact with are often good showcase projects. Projects that involve the development of the corporate human resources site or e-mail system, for example, may not have the most critical usability challenges, but they include applications used by almost everyone in the company. This means that good usability work will be widely experienced and very visible. While good design may not be noticed (good design has a way of seeming comfortable, proper, and forgettable), bad designs are memorable. You will need to point out the design features, insights, and advantages offered by the showcase project. With their attention drawn to the design, the corporate staff members will notice the difference.

Expectations

Once the showcase has been selected according to the criteria outlined in this chapter and properly staffed, the project is set up to succeed. The team members will follow the methodology and apply the standards, templates, and tools. Like test pilots, they will find things that do not work properly, and they will usually be able to manage the situation before there is a major crash.

The showcase team has a lot to manage. The project must continue with excellence as a demonstration of proper practice, use of the infrastructure, and the value of usability work. The methodology and standards must be fine-tuned. The communication links and organizational buy-in must be achieved. This is all a tall order. But the success of the showcase is essential to the continuation of institutionalization. You may have a beautiful aircraft on the drawing board, but a crash by the test pilot will certainly prevent immediate acceptance of the design.

Just as the test pilot must both fly the plane and gather the measurements required for aircraft certification, the showcase team must do the same. You can gather clear metrics from the showcase, including specific improvements in user experience and performance and the time required to do the user-centered work.

The showcase project is tough. It is the first project of its kind in a new environment, and it may be difficult to translate the time you invested and the usability metrics to a business analysis. You can calculate the ROI of the showcase project, but the results might not—in fact, should not—be representative. Typically, there are too many unusual challenges in a showcase to make the results indicative of other projects. The value of the showcase project is in the testing and refining of the process and infrastructure, not just in the ROI of that particular project.

Finally, create a presentation to tell the story of the showcase project. This presentation needs to be shared around the organization. It can become a great sales piece for institutionalization and can also provide lessons learned and present remaining needs. This presentation provides the impetus for the ongoing full institutionalization effort.

Your showcase project provides the real-world demonstration of the value of your initial institutionalization efforts. It is the tangible effort that the usability supporters in your company can look to for proof that their commitment has been well placed. However, because it can also be the scapegoat for those within the organization who are looking for an excuse to stand up against usability, its importance cannot be underestimated. Invest as much time, quality staff, and additional resources as possible into making your showcase a success. The next chapter outlines some of the organizational details necessary to establish an effective usability staff.

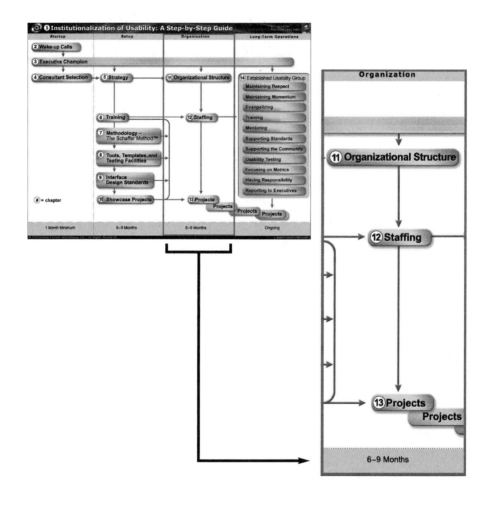

Part III

Organization

Once you have a proper infrastructure in place and a full understanding of your organization's needs, it makes sense to build a usability team. This usability team can be structured in many ways, and it is important to find the right structure to meet these needs and to place the people in the correct parts of the overall organization.

In the end, the success of the usability effort depends very much on the quality and appropriateness of the staff recruited to do the work. Without skilled staff, the infrastructure will be of little benefit. Take care in assembling your team.

In the Organization phase, the benefits of usability work can begin to accumulate. You can start to make usability a competitive differentiator and can expect to see usability become routine. The projects can begin in earnest, bringing new challenges of scheduling and testing your organization's ability to work smart with limited resources.

Chapter 11

Organizational Structure

➤ Spread usability consciousness throughout the organization. The focus on usability cannot reside only within a single group or team. In order to succeed, the idea of the importance of usability must permeate the entire organization's awareness and processes.

➤ Three types of organizational structures are commonly considered for the permanent usability team.

- *Matrix*—There is a central usability group, but that group does not do all the work. The central group also supports usability practitioners working within different project teams. This structure works well for medium- and large-sized organizations.

- *Centralized*—All the usability staff members are in a single team and are assigned temporarily to help on specific projects as needed. This structure works well for small organizations.

- *Decentralized*—Usability staff members are allocated to specific projects and report up through the various lines of business. This structure has some inherent flaws; I don't recommend using it.

> All organizations need a central usability team. Although this team in reality is often found in many parts of the organization, it ideally exists under a Chief User Experience Officer (CXO) or the head of marketing.

> Have an effective escalation pathway in place for problems with funding, staffing, and even specific design decisions.

> Graphic artists, writers, and other usability-oriented staff may best be placed in the same organization as the central usability team.

The single most important organizational principle is that *usability does not reside in a single group.* Even if you have a team with that title, usability must permeate the organization.

Compare this situation with the health care model. In a health care organization, there are surgeons, doctors, paramedics, and nurses. All these people wear the "health care professional" title, have lots of technology and training at their disposal, and watch for the latest research findings and tools. This is the official health care organization, but every other person is a part of the health care system as well because they all have a basic level of understanding and appreciation of health issues. Just as everyone must be responsible to some extent for his or her own health, all employees should also be aware of and feel responsible for usability issues.

It has been common in the past to drop a usability team into an organization and hope that this strategy will work. This is like dropping a small group of well-meaning doctors into a foreign country where they don't speak the language. Let's consider the challenges. The usability team has its own jargon and perspective, and this can lead to communication problems with the developers. Usability professionals may talk about "personas," "scenarios," and "affordance design," and the developers won't have a clue what these terms mean. Because of the communications problems and differences in perspectives, the development community does not trust the usability staff.

With this lack of communication, the usability team often sees problems only when it is too late to fix them. This is a universal symptom of an incomplete institutionalization program. Developers are not sensitized to usability issues, so they do not realize there is a problem until users reject the application, or they find that the performance measurements are dismal. Developers proceed to create interfaces without knowing the basics of good design. They don't gather data from users, model and optimize the user's taskflow, apply research-based principles of good design, or do routine usability testing starting early in the project. Given the practices of many development organizations, it is no surprise that they build sites that aren't usable. Usability teams may feel helpless and ineffective in the wake of poor designs and end up clamoring for resources to fix the broken interfaces. The solution requires a proactive approach: The routine practices and perspectives have to change throughout the organization.

The objective of the institutionalization effort is to ensure the usability of all new sites and applications. This can be achieved only through a usability assurance system. When you consider implementation of this system, keep in mind that it should encompass the entire development organization, just as the health care system encompasses everyone in the community. Without this perspective, you will not have a successful usability institutionalization program, and the usability team will be ineffective.

I've participated in hundreds of meetings to plan the ideal organization for usability work. There are many nuances to the optimal structure, communication, and task allocation, but really only one organization works well for large companies—there needs to be a small centralized usability organization that supports usability practitioners who work in specific lines of business and are assigned to specific projects. For smaller organizations, the central usability team may be able to support the infrastructure and complete all the usability work. This chapter discusses these organizational structures, the issues of escalating problems, and how the usability team can work with usability-related groups.

Organizational Structures for Usability Teams

You need to establish a structure for the permanent usability organization. However, the goodwill and power of the people involved have as much or more impact on the success of usability as the structure does. Air traffic controllers manage an amazingly complex task and occasionally handle crises where lives are at stake. Their systems are antiquated, but they make the process work. Any structure can be made to work; people can work out informal networks of support and scavenge resources. Any structure can also be made to fail; if people decide not to accept the user-centered approach, they can sabotage it.

This said, it still makes sense to select an organizational structure that makes success more likely. Three types of organizations are commonly considered: decentralized, matrix, and centralized structures. Let's briefly consider each.

Decentralized Structure

This structure allocates all the usability staff members to specific projects, and people report up through the various lines of business. This seems wonderful because the staff members really become a part of the design groups. However, the structure almost always fails in the long run because there is no central group to provide a coherent set of methodology, standards, facilities, and consultative support or to provide a unified message to the executives. The practitioners are not supported by a usability-focused leader, so they often end up doing software testing or some other activity needed to meet a project date. The usability effort thus loses focus.

Matrix Structure

A matrix solution works well in mid- and large-sized companies. In this structure, there is a small central usability team as well as usability practitioners who work on projects and report to the various lines of business. The usability staff members are integrated and accepted within the project team, and they become deeply aware of the usability issues and tricks that apply to their areas of interest. This situation is very powerful, but there must also be a small central usability team to support the usability practitioners on the project teams.

As the dotted arrow in Figure 11-1 indicates, the central usability group has a reporting arrangement with the practitioners on the project teams. The practitioners have a secondary reporting pathway, with the usability leader providing career counseling and input on performance reviews. The central group works with practitioners on the project teams. The central team members are responsible for methods, tools, facilities, training, and sponsorship. They help select new staff, advocate for usability practitioners when there are conflicts, and provide ongoing consultative support and mentoring. Without a strong central team, the institutionalization effort will fail.

The central usability team must have a strong leader. The connections, political skills, and charisma of this central leader are vastly important. In addition, the central usability staff (see Chapter 12) needs to include strong technical experts in the area of usability who can update the standards, coach development teams, and operate as

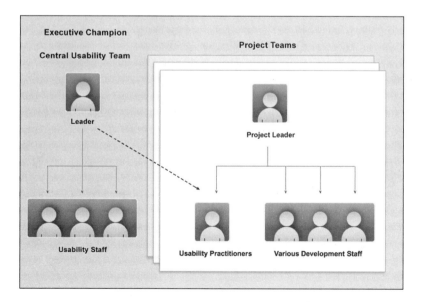

Figure 11-1: *A Matrix Solution for a Large Organization*

internal consultants. It is common for organizations with a central usability group to have three to five people working full time to support the methodology and consult with project teams. The team may also include a usability testing group that finds test participants and runs the testing rooms and equipment. This group would include one or two people prepared to customize this process as well as other staff qualified to run tests.

For a large organization, this matrix structure seems to work universally. This central group maintains momentum and provides a cohesive strategy. The group doesn't have to be very large, but it is essential to have one in place.

Centralized Structure

A centralized structure with all the usability staff in a single organization works well in smaller companies or in companies that have only a few development projects each year. In this structure, staff members are assigned to work on specific projects, and it is relatively easy to maintain the user-centered perspective of the staff members, upgrade their skill sets, and maintain the infrastructure needed for usability work.

This centralized usability team is responsible for maintaining the methods and standards, arranging training, and doing the actual project work. This is manageable only because there is a more limited span of activities and less need for coordination. The project teams are probably less cohesive, and someone from the central group may be better accepted in large organizations with insulated project teams that work together on a single program for years.

As with the matrix structure with a central usability team, the success of this one usability team greatly depends on the team's leadership. The team must maintain its political position and influence, as well as its infrastructure.

Being on Projects

By Colin Hynes, Director of Site Usability, Staples

A lot of making usability work is frankly just making sure we're on project teams. We are involved early in the process of every project on Staples.com, and part of our goal for next year is to do that throughout the catalog, corporate applications, and retail applications. We are "on the streets" with them—whether they're merchants, or marketing folks, or IS development folks, or creative graphics people—showing our value to each project on a day-to-day basis. We don't swoop in and say, "Here's all the stuff that's wrong with your catalog, your application, your Web site, and good luck fixing it—we'll see you in another two months when we can do the same thing." We're integrated as part of the team.

I'm actually a business owner on some of those projects. For example, we're redesigning the registration process on Staples.com. I'm the business owner of that—I'm the client of that project as well as being the usability guy. So the usability group owns some of the action. We're not just staff advisors; we're responsible for some of the projects.

Placement of a Central Team in the Overall Organization

A centralized usability team provides central coordination, infrastructure, and support. This team must reside in a given part of the overall organization and report to an executive champion who will support that group long-term. I have seen this team placed within quality assurance, within IT, and within the marketing department, but none of these solutions seem ideal. Placement under a CXO is the best positioning within a company. The subsections that follow briefly discuss these options.

Placement within Quality Assurance

The quality assurance group seems to be selected as a home for the usability team when usability is seen primarily as a testing function. Usually, the quality assurance team is out of the direct control of the IT organization to ensure that quality is independent and not compromised by the pressures the IT group faces in getting work done under tough time constraints. This is a good rationale from the viewpoint of usability testing.

By placing the usability team within the quality assurance group, it gains the characteristics of an auditor. This is wonderful for the summative usability testing process. The group can report tests of overall experience and performance with impunity. The group members may also be able to do consulting work with the detachment that should be characteristic of an auditing organization. In some ways, this is an attractive solution, but it can also be too separated from the direct business imperatives. This placement can cause the team to be focused on the ability of the design teams to pass a set of arbitrary usability metrics. The usability team may lose sight of the real business objectives (e.g., making money) as it focuses on the ability of the design teams to meet a set of bureaucratic requirements. One solution is to have a small, specialized usability testing group within the quality assurance organization and then assign the central group elsewhere.

Placement within IT

Many usability teams are placed directly within the IT organization. They are certainly considered systems development staff, so this seems reasonable. The usability team members report to the CIO or more often to a second-level executive in the systems development division. This type of placement makes sense, but it is profoundly dependent on the goodwill of the IT organization and therefore sometimes works poorly. If the executive champion is within the IT department, the placement of usability within IT may work very well. But if the executive champion works primarily in a different department, IT may be a tough place for the usability team to reside.

The IT organization may well be focused on two main goals: meeting the schedule and eliminating bugs. The IT group members often consider themselves successful if they get the site or application up in the time allotted. If the facility does not crash or have major errors in calculation, they celebrate a success. IT staff members are often bewildered by users who say, "That may be what we asked for, but it is not what we want." When they hear this complaint, they blame the users. If this is the character of the IT group, you cannot have an effective usability team in that setting.

Placement within Marketing

The central usability group is also sometimes put into the marketing organization. The marketing organization is focused on making money—a goal it accomplishes by satisfying customers. The marketing group generally has a strategy for moving the company ahead and has identified a market niche, a unique selling proposition, and a brand. The usability professionals then make sure that the sites and applications support this strategy. Usability professionals ensure that the technology is designed to be practical, meet the users' needs, and accommodate their limitations.

Marketing staff members quickly realize that the usability process is the logical continuation of their work. Sometimes the people in marketing try to take on the role of usability practitioner. If they receive training and certification this works well, but if they attempt to fill this role without training, it will be hard for them to be successful. In the best scenario, the marketing organization becomes the greatest promoter of usability engineering.

Of the current most common options—quality assurance, IT, or marketing—the best location for the central usability organization is usually within marketing. The marketing organization has a vested interest in the quality of user experience, and the marketing staff members want to ensure that IT provides real value. They are determined to use the IT expenditures in ways that really add value to customers. The usability team supports this process. In a sense, the usability engineering work is wholly focused on realizing marketing's vision. The usability practitioners ensure that the marketing strategy is carried forward through the detailed design of the site or application.

Organizations without a formal marketing department, such as government agencies, may find their usability personnel distributed to various groups. However, more and more of these agencies now have entities that are very similar to commercial product management or lines of business. Divisions in government that are focused on specific functional objectives are an appropriate part of the organization for usability staff—with the IT department as a last resort.

However, a few aspects of placing the usability team within the marketing organization still may prove challenging. First, some marketing organizations do not take a large view of customer interactions. They primarily are focused on advertising programs that create offers for customers, but they really don't think much about what is offered. They don't consider the customers' taskflows or process while determining their offers and getting them fulfilled. In this type of environment, the usability work will be a poor fit for the marketing organization. Even if the marketing team members do have a wider view, their expertise and focus is not usually on design and delivery. They set the direction for the products, but then they primarily are concerned with how to get customers to the point of sale. The issues of customer experience go on from there into product setup, normal usage, and problem management—this is not the main focus of most conventional marketing organizations.

Most marketing groups are responsible for more than just the online customer interaction. They must consider many channels of marketing communication and the customer's behavior within a store, through the mail, and during interaction with company staff. In general, this is a good thing: Usability work should be synchronized with the other modalities of interaction. Usability professionals do not design store layouts—marketers and consumer psychologists do this—but synchronization is important. Problems can occur if there is too little concern about the online experience. So if the marketing organization does not have a significant attachment to the online activities, it is a poor home for the usability group.

There is a second area of concern with marketing groups—they may not be clear on where marketing expertise stops and usability work takes over. This is an understandable problem because both marketing and usability professionals gather data from customers, and both care about customer motivation and perspective. The key difference is that *the marketing group defines the target, and the usability group hits it.*

When members of a marketing group run group focus sessions, they are searching for a good product idea. They gather customer data to define the target market for the idea, and they work to define the exact brand perception and selling proposition. With these elements defined, the usability team does its work with the development staff to ensure that the functional specification works for the defined user target. The usability team structures an interface and guides graphic design to create the target brand perception. The usability team engineers the taskflow that fulfills the unique selling proposition.

There can be overlap within this process. The marketing group often provides the logo along with the color palettes and corporate typefaces that are known to support the brand and are being used in offline channels. The marketing group also often selects terms that describe a product offering, whether or not these terms mean anything to users. Marketing provides feature lists that may sometimes be a close match for the real user needs. At the same time, the usability team may discover issues with the brand values or presentation. The usability team may suggest different descriptions of an offering or at least highlight the ones that will not work. It is important to be cautious regarding the overlap in these areas to ensure that the process remains smooth. A good usability team makes a conscious effort to work with marketing throughout the process.

Another challenge with the marketing organization is that marketing may have almost no interest in systems that are not seen by customers. The usability team should work on the company intranet and customer service applications. It is certainly possible to have a separate usability team for internal applications, but it is a better use of resources to have a single usability group. This central group can then work on these projects. There is usually too much overlap in the work to be done on methodology, infrastructure, tools, and training to have separate usability teams.

Placement under a CXO

While challenges exist when placing the central usability team within the marketing organization, in general this is often the best current option. However, there is one other potential home—the promised land for usability staff—but it is currently mostly just a dream. The central usability team can be placed under the supervision of a CXO.

As of this writing, there are few CXOs in place, but the concept provides an ideal structure for the usability team. The CXO is placed high in the organization and has responsibility across every line of business. A single interaction with the user may call on several different divisions. Yet the CXO has the position, power, and responsibility to see that the interaction is a coherent success.

Once created, the role of CXO becomes one of the key positions in an organization's power structure. It is certainly a position that needs to be filled by an executive with considerable savvy and vision. The

An Executive Must Champion Usability

By Harley Manning, Research Director, Forrester Research

Almost every time we research organizational issues (including how the project is run), we find a project owner matrix-managing a cross-functional team. This project owner needs an executive champion who can make sure that he or she gets funding and gets support against all the organizational sniping that goes on. This executive champion should report to either the head of the division or the CEO. If not, the project has the potential to get derailed by efforts from other groups.

And it's just as important for the champion to know what not to do as it is to know what to do. If you are an executive, it's important not to play other roles.

head of marketing has the responsibility of getting people engaged with the organization's products; the CXO is responsible for good things happening to the customer throughout that engagement. This is a huge responsibility and one that is best placed with a single person who can oversee the entire range of engagements. For more information on the role of the CXO, see Chapter 3.

Escalation of Problems

When positioning the usability team, be sure to consider the chain of escalation for problems. With a new institutionalization effort, there are sure to be clashes, including problems with funding, staffing, and even specific design decisions. There may also be some stubborn vice president who feels that a wiggly animation will really improve sales—especially accompanied by a short and continuously looping music track. The project teams can bring these types of problems to the central usability group, and the leader of the central group can try to resolve issues. Usually, a composite video of users complaining about download time and annoyance with the design convinces the well-intentioned executive. However, this approach does not always work. So what should the appropriate escalation path be? This is a critical question.

The CXO is the ideal path for escalation. Only the CXO has unambiguous responsibility for the user experience and a position high enough in the organization to successfully resolve these types of issues. Without the escalation path to the CXO in place, there is a potential for problems. A usability group in marketing may clash with the senior executive who has strong design ideas. A usability group in IT may clash with the executive who just wants to get the site up on time, regardless of user issues. A usability group embroiled in design problems may get little help from a manager who is responsible for writing procedures, best practices, or quality assurance reports. The escalation path will go up through the area where the central usability group has been situated. If this is not under a CXO, it may be in marketing, IT, quality assurance, and so on. But the pathway of escalation must be credible and effective.

The leader of the usability team should strive to resolve issues directly, but there must be a plausible and effective escalation pathway. This is the primary reason why the leader needs to report high in the organization. Otherwise, user issues will rarely win out over issues of schedule, politics, habit, and preference.

Graphic Artists, Writers, and Other Usability-Oriented Staff

A wide family of specialists helps form the actual user experience. For example, graphic artists create icons and other graphical images, technical writers generate content, and market research groups get wider and different data about users. How do all these different types of people interact within the organization?

If you have a CXO, you have someone in a unified position who can coordinate the disparate central groups that focus on user experience. The market researchers can raise issues to be studied by the usability team, and the usability specialists can bring challenges to the graphics team. There is an opportunity for a powerful creative synergy. If you don't have a CXO, you need to consider placing these staff members in your central usability group.

Despite the fact that they are not usability specialists, these other staff members have a critical role in supporting the usability engineers and/or the creation of a positive user experience.

The single most important organizational principle is that *the concern for usability should not reside only in a single group.* Whether or not there will be a team with that title, concern for usability must permeate the organization. The structure you choose should be appropriate to the size and goals of your organization and should also take into account the best placement of the central usability team. The next chapter provides information on effective staffing theories and strategies to help complete the structure you have established.

Chapter 12

Staffing

➤ The manager of the central usability group is the day-to-day leader of the central organization and also manages the overall progress of usability in the company. It is better to have a good manager without much usability experience than a usability expert who does not understand management.

➤ The central usability group needs usability professionals who play a number of types of roles. You may need to staff all of these roles:

- Internal consultant
- Documenter
- Specialist
- Researcher

➤ Usability practitioners do the actual usability work—they are generalists in usability engineering with a solid skill set for doing the design process. In small companies, they may be a part of the central usability organization. In larger companies, they should generally report to the project teams within each line of business.

➤ Using an offshore model is a potential partial solution for almost any organization building its usability staff.

This chapter describes the staff roles needed for the institutionalization of usability and what to look for when hiring people to fill these roles. The concept of roles does not necessarily map directly to job descriptions because one person may fulfill a number of roles. Conversely, one role may be filled by several individuals. You can mix and match people's jobs and roles as necessary, but the roles must be staffed. In a very large organization, there tends to be more specialization and more likelihood that several people will work on a given role. In smaller companies, the roles condense so that a single individual must handle multiple roles. For example, in very small company with only one usability engineer, that person may need to fulfill *all* the roles described in this chapter (a daunting requirement), while a medium-sized company might have a specialist in cross-cultural design who also has graphic art skills.

Earlier chapters discussed developing the infrastructure of the usability operation. As a result, you now have the knowledge necessary to create a "usability factory" complete with appropriate processes and tools. But the success of the factory very much depends on getting the right usability staff in place, and this is not an easy task. Only a limited number of educational institutions offer graduate programs for software usability practitioners, and many graduates of these programs still need real-world experience.[1] At the undergraduate level, there are some courses available in usability but not degrees that focus on the necessary skills. Many countries are developing practitioner programs to meet this rising demand; thus, an offshore model is another potential option for organizations to consider. In this chapter, I share insights gained during two decades of experience with hiring usability staff.

The Chief User Experience Executive

Once the institutionalization effort has succeeded, a central usability organization should be in place (as discussed in Chapter 11). This organization reports to an executive, who may be a Chief User

---

1. For a listing of the current university programs available, see www.humanfactors.com/downloads/degrees.asp.

Experience Officer (CXO), the senior vice president of marketing, or the head of quality assurance. Whatever the title or position, this executive has a set of activities and responsibilities to fulfill.

In many ways, the user experience executive continues the role of the executive champion (refer to Chapter 3 for additional details on this role). It is essential to continue chanting the mantra of the business focus for the usability work and to continue working within the politics of the organization to ensure the support from key players. In some ways, these tasks are much easier to address now that the organization has been sensitized to usability issues and a foundation of support is in place. The initial strategy of institutionalization has given way to a far more complex set of projects and initiatives, and the executive must guide the balance between strategic activities, infrastructure, and tactical work. In addition, the executive still needs to continuously monitor progress, solve problems, and celebrate success.

During times of growth and prosperity, there may be little concern about maintaining the usability team. But during difficult times, the executive must have a solid case for continuation of the team. In the past, the usability organization was often cut early in a downturn—this can be discouraging for usability staff, and many talented people have left the field because of this. The executive needs to inspire a sense of purpose, commitment, and security in the organization.

No matter if you have just one usability practitioner or thousands, you still need someone at an executive level playing the role of executive champion. The executive champion was critical in starting the process for institutionalizing usability, and a champion will be critical for continuing and maintaining usability engineering practices. If you have a CXO, this person is most likely your executive champion. If you do not have a CXO, you need to clarify who your executive champion is.

The Central Usability Organization Manager

The executive champion or the chief user experience executive provides high-level strategy and support. This role is essential, but the daily work falls under the control of the manager of the central usability organization, who has a very different job than that of the executives. The role requires at least a good understanding of usability technology, along with very good connections in the organization. While the executive might spend a small part of his or her time on usability, the central usability organization manager is fully dedicated to the control and promotion of the usability engineering capability within the organization.

The central usability group has a whole agenda of projects and services for which the executive champion may provide overall direction, but the manager has to plan, fund, staff, and monitor each one. This is a lot like running an internal consulting group—there is an infrastructure to maintain and a set of project offerings to design, create, market, and deliver.

The manager of the usability team is sure to spend a substantial amount of time addressing personnel issues, hiring good usability staff, and cultivating them internally. The existing staff members also need to be mentored—the manager should dedicate time to developing career planning and feedback sessions for this group.

The ideal qualities for a usability manager include in-depth knowledge of usability engineering practices, a full grasp of the organizational dynamics, and a love of management. The best people to manage usability teams are high-powered usability experts with "street smarts" and an interest in management. They have the expertise to chart the course for usability work and contribute a great deal to the process. With in-depth understanding of organizational dynamics, even if they are not familiar with your organization, they will quickly learn about it. The ideal manager is fully committed to usability and won't easily be sidetracked into pitfalls.

If you cannot find or afford a "walk-on-water" usability expert with management skills, what should you do? You may be tempted to place in this job a highly skilled usability specialist who has a deep under-standing of the field. He or she will understand what needs to be accomplished, will be able to assess the quality of work, and can help make wise tradeoffs when difficult decisions arise. However, placing someone like this into the management position might lead to the end of the institutionalization effort. Without the necessary street smarts and political skills, the entire usability organization may be marginal-ized and eventually eliminated. Some organizational cultures may be more supportive of a technical expert placed in a leadership position. But for most organizations, the technical specialist is ill equipped to run with the wolves—or even successfully run from them.

As a second choice, select a street-smart manager who cares about usability issues and give him or her plenty of training and support. This person's understanding of the management role and channels of communication is the most important capability. If he or she pos-sesses a limited amount of usability engineering expertise, this is more manageable. The professional manager must be dedicated to usability and have the ability to build a team of experts. The manager must then have the ability to grow the team and protect it. Ideally, the manager can mentor the team members in content as well as clear roadblocks for them. If this is not possible, the manager may need to delegate content mentoring to another staff person or an out-side mentor. The management role is the most critical for the team.

There is a common idea that the manager of the central usability team can also complete the work of the executive champion, but this usually results from a lack of appreciation for the champion's criti-cal role. This is a major pitfall to avoid. You need a real executive to be the executive champion, and this role should not be combined with the central manager's job description. Refer to Chapter 3 for details on the role of the executive champion.

The Central Usability Organization Staff

As mentioned in the previous chapter, the central usability group is a small nucleus of staff members with usability expertise who coor-dinate usability activities for the company. This central group forms the dissemination point for best practices and success stories and should manage challenges in order to maintain progress toward an optimized user experience. This group rarely includes more than six to ten people. (In large organizations, additional staff members are distributed in project teams.) This central usability team is essential to keeping the institutionalization effort moving forward, staying coordinated, and remaining lively.

Four types of subroles may be needed within this team to complete the centralized support functions: (1) internal consultant, (2) documenter, (3) specialist, and (4) researcher. Similar to the concept of archetypes in mythology, a bit of each role usually exists in every usability specialist, although there are also people who function well in only a limited set of areas. Some people can perform only one of these roles well. Every central organization needs an internal consultant and a documenter, but only larger organizations can afford a specialist or justify much research.

The Internal Consultant

People in the role of internal consultant reach out to mentor many different junior usability staff members and provide selective support on many projects. Junior usability staff members have a lot to manage. They are often doing activities like data gathering and testing for the first time, and they need moral support while they build confidence. It is hard to walk into a testing facility and face your first test participant—there is always a fear that you will not be able to manage the participants. In fact, this fear is somewhat well founded. Some test participants wander off on tangents unmercifully. Others are very angry about something the company did and want to talk about nothing but that one erroneous item on their bill, for example. The consultant often accompanies the junior usability staff members for a few sessions until their confidence builds.

Aside from emotional support, there is a real need for an infusion of technical expertise. Often, a few moments of attention from the consultant help the junior professional avoid weeks of unnecessary work and avert real dangers to the design quality. If the internal consultant takes just a moment to notice that the task analysis documentation is too detailed and to provide the junior staff with appropriate feedback, this can save weeks of otherwise wasted effort. Noticing that the design concept requires impossible technology or could be accomplished with a simple and standard page type can also avert future rework. The internal consultant plays a key role in developing technical expertise through his or her guidance.

Fulfilling the requirements of this role is generally great fun. An internal consultant gets to make a positive impact in lots of arenas but rarely has to stay to complete what is sometimes considered the hard and boring detailed work. It is the ideal job for the more aggressive and highly skilled usability expert.

It is essential to have high-quality technical skills for this role. Internal consultants have to plan projects and suggest designs ideas without time for analysis and reflection. They have to be definitive, and these consultants cannot afford to be wrong very often. Concurrently, consultants should also be emissaries for the usability initiative. Internal consultants must constantly educate the organization about the value of usability and the resources available in the organization. Like an external consultant from a usability vendor's organization, internal consultants have to create positive impressions and bonds.

The Documenter

The documenter role within the usability engineering staff is far less proactive than the role of consultant or specialist. The documenter spends much less time interacting with the constituent project teams. Instead, he or she carefully crafts the tools and templates needed to complete the usability work and then creates and updates the infrastructure.

A lot of this type of documentation needs to be done. The documenter updates the methodology to reflect the new practices, lessons learned, and standards documentation with new screen types and enhanced rules. The documenter must maintain the reusable templates for test questionnaires and deliverable documents. The documenter needs to be a detail-oriented individual skilled in technical writing who will do an excellent job of keeping track of documents.

The Specialist

The need for a specialist role depends on the type of work the company does. There are many types of specialists in the usability engineering field. Software usability is a specialty within the overall field of usability engineering. Most usability people work within the fields of transportation, military equipment, consumer products, aviation, and so on. But within software usability engineering, there are numerous subspecialties. If your organization's core competency involves one of these subspecialties, it may make sense to hire a usability professional with expertise in this particular area. Below are some of the more common areas of specialization within the field of user-centered software engineering.

The Technology Specialist

Some usability specialists attend to particular types of software technology. These experts may specialize in Web applications, GUIs, voice response systems (both touch tone and voice recognition), and handheld units. There is a lifetime's worth of detail in each of these areas. For example, a good general practitioner or consultant knows the basics of a good voice response script and knows how to make menus short and simple. But there are complex strategies for tuning the voice recognition algorithm; even the way that the software determines the end of a word is challenging [Kotelly 2003]. If the core business of the organization involves voice recognition software, for example, it is very worthwhile to have staff specialists who understand these nuances. If, however, this is an occasional specialized area of need, it is best to find a specialist to hire on a contract basis.

The User and Domain Specialists

Specialists focus on particular domains or user types. Some focus just on the design of software for children, on financial applications, or on the presentation of graphic models for oil drilling. Every domain has its own language, insights, and challenges. While it is true that a good consultant can make a positive impact on almost any application, there is real value in hiring someone who has experience in the domain. So if the company is wholly focused on building gaming software, it pays to have a specialist familiar with the gaming industry, environment, and customer populations.

The same developmental activities are needed. You cannot just go to the specialist and say, "You have been building gaming applications for 30 years, so make one for me." This approach can at best result in the duplication of the design, business strategy, unique selling proposition, and branding of a previous client. The specialist must go through a full user-centered design process. This ensures generation of a design that precisely fits your organization's competitive strategy. The specialist's expertise helps save time in understanding the domain and improves the quality of questions. This expertise also helps avoid pitfalls and accommodates design requirements that may not be obvious. But the full design process is needed to create a competitive design.

The Developmental Activity Specialist

A good general practitioner or consultant in the field can complete the full range of developmental activities in the user-centered methodology. However, some people really specialize in a limited part of the development life cycle. For example, some people may specialize in conducting usability testing. Developmental activity specialists are often less expensive than generalists because the specialists' skill set is limited. These specialists may be very useful as members of project teams. They may also be collected in a service organization within the central usability group—this is a way to use the group's specialty more cost effectively. You can apply their work across many projects throughout your organization.

Other Specialists

The expensive specialists are more appropriately placed within the central usability team. These experts have a really in-depth understanding of how to perform a given task or manage a specific aspect of development. For example, all trained usability consultants are sensitive to the issues of globalization and localization of software and are aware of the challenges within this area. For example, a well-trained consultant for an American company would never approve the name "Morning Mist" for a perfume product destined for sales in Germany (where *mist* means *manure*).

Also, these specialists may know principles of design that make translation easier, such as, "Do not embed variables in a sentence that will be translated because the syntax changes will shift the order of the variables, making the rendering of the translated sentences hard to code and maintain." For example, a sentence like, "Thanks, [username]! That is [units bought] [color] [product] added to your account" would translate correctly as, "Gracias, [username]! Eso es [units bought] [product] [color] agregado a su cuenta," causing the programmer to need to reverse the sequence of color and product.

The generalist can do a credible job of avoiding many pitfalls in cross-cultural design. However, specialists in the field spend their professional lives understanding the issues and processes of localization and have models that identify the key differences between cultures that may impact the design. They know characteristics of the target culture that will be of special concern.

Cross-cultural design specialists know how to check the practicality of the application's taskflow in the new culture. They know how to create a translation package to guide the conversion process and how to guide developers to code for different character sets and field formats. If your organization is designing applications or sites in many different countries and cultures, it makes sense to have an expert in this field. If your organization is designing for a limited set of cultures, it makes sense to have specialists only within those cultures. It is wonderful to have natives from target regions working as usability staff members or at least people fluent in the different languages. This does not mean they can skip data gathering and testing, but they will have a much easier time running the studies.

If your business is defined by having a certain expertise, you will benefit from having one of the numerous types of usability specialists on board. Besides the specialists listed above, there are specialists in such areas as multidimensional data, visualization methods, online search strategies, design for disabled people, security, and font design. While it is important not to expect a specialist to be able to play a more generalist role within the usability team, if your organization is faced with a very specialized domain, it may make sense to have a specialist on board.

The Researcher

Another type of role within the central usability group is the researcher. Many university professors and students work on usability studies of Web sites and software applications, and a few organizations still fund this type of research. One type of applied research may be worthwhile to invest in within the central usability teams of most large organizations. These organizations may gain significant competitive advantages if they can solve certain usability problems. For example, a company may need to know the effect of menu design strategy on the time it takes to find an item. If the user knows the word and must find it within a list of 18 items, how long will it take if the list is random, alphabetical, or grouped by function? In most cases, you can just look up the answers from research that has already been completed.[2] But in other cases, you may need to complete the research yourself. Much of this analysis will be completed as a part of testing by the project teams, but carefully researched solutions to general research questions that apply to many of the organization's applications will add value on many projects. The more applied, specific, and immediate the question, the more appropriate it is to answer the question within the organization.

If you are going to have a researcher in your group, make sure to hire someone with education and experience in conducting research studies. A background in experimental psychology, for example, is beneficial. He or she should also be accustomed to working in an applied setting because the research you want to conduct is usually not going to be theoretical.

---

2. For example, Card [1982] found it took users 3.23 seconds to find a word on a randomized list, .81 seconds for an alphabetical list, and 1.28 seconds for a functional list.

The Usability Manager and Practitioners

In small organizations, the central group lends usability specialists to projects. In medium and large organizations, practitioners work for lines of business and are assigned to specific projects. The project team may have only a single usability person, but really two different roles must be provided: a management role and a working practitioner's role. The manager is really the project manager for the usability activity. Fulfilling this role means creating a plan for the usability work within the project. The company methodology lays out a generic project plan, but it is up to the manager to mold that plan and elect the specific activities and level of resources to make the generic methodology fit with the project time frame, budget, and key objectives. This takes a lot of creativity and experience. It requires a top-level staff person with advanced degrees, certifications, and a proven track record. This person must address many issues and business decisions.

HFI has seen that an experienced project team manager with good planning skills can cut as much as 10–15% from the time and effort of the usability work. A poor planning job, however, makes a usability project fail. Project planning is not composed of a single activity. Rather, it must be refined and revisited throughout the process. Project planning for usability work is mostly about finding shortcuts and avoiding traps, and the project team manager is instrumental in making this happen. The following list gives a sense of the level of planning considerations required.

- The manager decides to skip an initial usability test. The current application is obviously bad. Everyone knows it. So the manager decides to skip an initial usability test on the current application and go right to the design phases. This shortcut saves $50,000 and three weeks of time.

- The manager is told that users are hard to find but still does not agree to gather data with internal users. The internal staff, interviewed as surrogate users, would be polluted with the company viewpoint, and several features might appear to be desired that are in fact of no interest to the real users. Avoiding this trap saves $250,000 in unneeded development and coding.

- During a project team discussion about the best width of the text, the team members say they want to run a study to find the answer. The manager recalls seeing research, looks it up, and puts an end to the discussion with a clear recommendation for a 100-character-wide display. This saves the team another two days of fighting and prevents an unnecessary study. This short-cut saves three weeks and $30,000 to do the research.
- The team wants to immediately begin doing detailed design on pages and concurrently coding them. The manager forces the team to make standard templates and reusable code. This decreases the final development time by three weeks and also avoids customer complaints due to inconsistent and idiosyn-cratic designs. Avoiding this trap saves three weeks and $80,000. Also, there are increased sales due to improvements in customer perceptions.
- The key business objective is to make the site self-evident. So instead of employing random or stratified sampling, the man-ager decides to just study low-end users. Instead of studying 50 users, the team can test with just 20 users and get better data. This shortcut saves four days of time and $15,000.

Between avoiding traps and finding shortcuts, a good project team manager uses his or her experience to save the company time and money.

In the absence of a strong central usability manager, the project team manager may have to build the team. This means recruiting and screening the right staff for the group, attending to the career devel-opment needs and personal motivation of the team members, and mentoring and growing the staff.

Finally, on an ongoing basis, the manager has to support the proj-ect's progress. He or she must lead the difficult negotiations with the other developers, track project milestones, unsnarl logistics, and allocate staff resources. Constant interactions with the other devel-opment team members are required, and adjustments in schedule must be made to accommodate them.

The project team manager role must be staffed by someone who really understands the usability engineering process. The project planning is the toughest part of this role, and it is possible to get help for planning from the central usability team. But even if assistance is provided for the management of the project plan, the execution of the plan requires someone who knows the details and vicissitudes of usability work. The person responsible for the usability of the project should complete the project planning. This is not the CXO, the executive champion, or even the usability team manager. This type of project management involves managing a specific project, not the usability group as a whole.

The Creative Director and the Graphic Designer

Traditionally, usability engineers work mostly to make practical, useful, and usable designs. However, achieving these goals is often not enough. Don Norman, one of the great thinkers in the usability field, has described how design must go beyond usability [Norman 2002]. Designs must be satisfying, pleasant, inspiring, entertaining, and beautiful. This is the new frontier of the usability field, but usability staff members are often ill equipped to reach this goal on their own—this requires combining usability work with graphic design.

For projects where the design must appeal to the user's emotions, creative and artistic functional roles must be built into the project along with the usability roles. The degree of involvement and importance varies. If the site is an online brochure, the usability staff may have little to do, but the graphic design staff may have a great deal of work to do on the creative design and presentation. Conversely, within a human resources site designed for an intranet, there may be very little creative work necessary. In this example, users may only want to see their 401K and benefits. Therefore, there needs to be a pleasant graphic skin on the site that supports the company's brand, but expenditures on aesthetic work should be limited. However, in most projects, there will need to be a mix and balance of these two perspectives. Public Web sites and shrink-wrap applications are both examples of projects that need a wise balance between usability engineering and creative design.

Creative directors and graphic designers make sites and applications that are innovative. However, the problem with innovative

designs is that they are usually hard to use because they tend to operate in unexpected ways. In contrast, usability engineers make designs
that are conventional and therefore easy to use, but these designs are
often not inspiring, entertaining, and beautiful. Therefore, to reach
the objective of a cool *and* usable design, a synergistic effort needs to
bring the creative and usability engineering perspectives together.
Figure 12-1, created by Dr. John Sorflaten of HFI, illustrates this pull
between cool and conventional in design.

To make a site more attractive, there must be a functional role for the
creative director and the graphic designer. These people come from
visual arts and design backgrounds, and many have also come into
interactive design from advertising backgrounds. The creative director generally develops the concepts for the design, while the graphic
designer does the physical drawing and creates alternative designs
to meet the objectives of the creative director. The graphic designer
is responsible for decisions such as color palettes and font families.
If you have a site that must be inspiring, entertaining, and beautiful,
you need skilled people playing this role.

Integration of the usability effort and the creative design effort is
sometimes tricky. These groups have different perspectives and

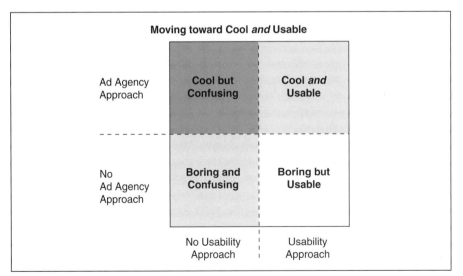

Figure 12-1: *Dr. John Sorflaten's Matrix of Usability and Creativity*
(see Plate 4)

methods, and they may not agree on the design. In a worst-case situation, both groups want to control the interface structure, standard templates, and final page designs.

When bringing together these two separate viewpoints, you need to manage the situation. First, each side needs to become sensitive to what the other is trying to accomplish. Then you need to negotiate clear boundaries and roles to make this collaboration succeed. The right solution depends on the type of application being designed. Let's examine in greater depth two of the examples mentioned earlier in this chapter.

If your organization is designing an online brochure, there is little need for complex interactivity; user speed and accuracy are also of less importance. Therefore, hire a creative director to run the project. The usability team can check the designs to make sure there are no obvious points of confusion and perhaps run a usability test to check that there are no places where the user gets lost or frustrated. But the focus of the project is really on the creative design.

A different situation is building a site for employees to set up benefit elections on the intranet. This task requires more interactions. The users are not interested in being entertained by the site—they just want to be able to get the job done quickly. In this case, let the usability team determine its process, and have a graphic artist complete a basic treatment of the design—there is little creative work to do.

You should also consider setting up an interdisciplinary team in which a usability engineer, graphic designer, and technical writer work together as equals. The usability engineer is responsible for navigation and interaction, the graphic designer for the graphical elements, and the technical writer for writing and editing content.

Outside Consultants

Usability consultancies can provide staff that fit into many of the roles described in this chapter. But one unique role can be filled only by an outside vendor: Because the outside consultant is not a part of the organizational structure, he or she can act as impartial arbiter and facilitator. This type of consultant can offer a unique set of services,

The Social Security Administration's Usability Team

By Sean Wheeler, Lead Usability Specialist,
The Social Security Administration

We currently have 18 people on the Usability Center staff at the Social Security Administration (SSA). Half of the staff members have their master's degrees, and one holds a Ph.D. More important than title, their training is consistent in areas directly related to usability. In addition to academic credentials, they typically brought 7 to 10 years of experience in "usability" when they joined our team.

We are a rather strange lot because our team is a well-integrated mixture of federal employees and contractors. Because the contractor staffing mechanism is available to us, the SSA Usability Center has team members with skills that would be impossible for us to obtain otherwise. As an example, we are able to do electronic prototyping within the Usability Center so we can get a reading on the accessibility of our designs early in the software development process—a high-value contribution to project teams within the federal government. Our federal staff members bring many years of experience as employees from SSA field offices with the corresponding knowledge of the laws and procedures of the agency as well as the needs and expectations of our customers that comes only from direct public contact work. This combination of skills has served us very well.

We are really expanding our scope now. We're a much different organization in 2003 than we were a few years ago. Today, most of our staff has been involved in user interface design and human factors work for 10 to 15 years, with much of that experience in the private sector. The team's skills allow us to support agency-wide process changes that put early focus on user needs and design rather than on the late-in-life-cycle usability testing we started with. This rapid infusion of skills allowed us to support project teams in ways that would have been impossible when the center was established in 1996.

and his or her impartiality can help break logjams while "saving face" for the internal staff.

The outside consultant can also communicate at any level of the organization. Within an organization, strong protocols usually prevent a staff member from walking into the CEO's office and raising unpleasant concerns. The consultant is permitted and encouraged (and paid) to be critical. This type of service is an important part of the institutionalization solution. For more details on this role, see Chapter 4.

What to Look for When Hiring

Hiring your first usability staff can be tricky. The market for usability personnel is poorly defined. The people responsible for recruiting and hiring in your organization may not have experience or guidance in what to look for.

An organization hiring senior people for the first time may have a hard time finding them. Senior practitioners in the usability field are still a small group, and they tend to be networked together with professional groups such as the ACM SIGCHI and the Usability Professionals Association.[3] For more junior staff, there are thousands of people in the field (and many thousands more who claim to be in the field).

Most companies have a very limited number of usability experts on staff; many companies do not have one person with the entire usability skill set described below. In many cases, the bulk of the usability staff may have to come from outside hires. But there is a danger in this practice. It is important to have the usability team be an integral part of the organization. It therefore helps to have staff members on the team who come from within the organization. If most of the usability staff members are outsiders, it may be very hard to get full acceptance of the team. This means it does make sense to use staff promoted from within the organization. The insiders understand the organization better and may fit in better than new hires.

---

3. For more information on ACM SIGCHI, visit www.acm.org/sigchi/. For more information on the Usability Professionals Association, visit www.upassoc.org.

The problem is that the insiders probably have very little usability engineering skill. Therefore, these people need a real commitment from management for training, mentoring, and consultative support.

If your organization is new to usability, consider using recruiters who specialize in usability staff. They will be familiar with the best people in the field and will know when someone is ready to move. They will also be able to help screen more junior staff. They should have full technical expertise and testing methods to make sure you get the people who best meet your needs. Once you have a core of experts in your organization, you may be able to have them work their networks, go to the usability engineering trade shows, and track potential new staff members.

Hiring usability staff is a big step that involves a huge investment in the form of salaries, benefits, management, facilities, and training. But these elements form only a small part of the risk. The far larger risk is in the opportunity cost for usable designs. The new employee will be responsible for the quality of the user experience and performance of many applications over time. If the person is a poor practitioner, these costs can easily dwarf his or her loaded labor rate. The skills and factors discussed in the following subsections are based on many years of experience in hiring usability staff.

Usability Skills for a General Practitioner

As mentioned earlier in the book, usability work is not just common sense. If it were, you could tell developers to pay attention and the designs would be successful. Yet without concrete usability skills, the developers create suboptimal designs.

A core philosophy and feeling for design is perhaps the most important prerequisite for a good usability professional. Usability professionals should have a user-oriented philosophy. This doesn't mean simply asking the customers what they want and giving it to them. This is a sign of an immature or ill-trained practitioner. Rather, you should hire someone who sees the user's needs and psyche as something to understand, to design for, and to support. The usability practitioner needs to be focused on the practical viewpoint of the user and on systematically bringing technology to the user's service. This is a style of operating, and it is important. To test for this, see how specialists react to the idea of a cool new technology that is clearly impractical for users. They may be polite about it, but there should be a feeling of disdain. Usability practitioners act as a protective shield for cool but impractical ideas in your projects. A bit of jaundiced skepticism is useful.

Usability staff must understand human behavior and be able to make good predictions of how users will react to and operate software. In a good training program, usability students read research articles and predict the results from the methodological description. In time, they will become pretty good at prediction; they will develop a sense for the things that confuse users and for the physical manipulations that are awkward. They will understand what makes users uncomfortable, angry, or confused and will be able to predict the time it takes to complete an operation or learn a procedure. These predictions may not necessarily be exact, but they will be pretty accurate.

A lot of design decisions are based on the ability of the usability specialist to quickly estimate user consequences. To get a sense of this, it is beneficial to have prospective staff members review some page designs to determine whether these people can quickly see the things that matter most. For example, I have often used a terrible clothing site design for this purpose. The site is organized by brand, so while shopping, the user has to identify the brand and then see all the different types of clothes from that manufacturer. Good prospective employees immediately see that the user needs the site to be organized by male and female categories and then by types of clothes.

Potential candidates need to have a good overall knowledge of the research and models within the field. Every usability practitioner needs many core understandings. Some facts should probably be "top of mind" for any good candidate. For example, the practitioner should immediately know that about 7% of men and 0.4% of women have some color weakness [Goldberg et al 1995]. They should know that all displays could be seen as a competition between the signal that the user should perceive and the surrounding noise [Rehder et al. 1995]. Usability practitioners should work to maintain a signal-to-noise ratio that gets the message through.

Usability practitioners should know that there are population stereotypes for how things work (e.g., in the United States, pushing a light switch up to turn on the lights) and that the stereotypes are different for different user populations (the English push the light switch *down* to turn on the lights). Practitioners should know that users see things in context and can make mistakes as a result. For example, if users expect to see a letter, a handwritten "13" can look like a "B." Users also make common keying errors, such as hitting the letter "o" instead of the number "0." Certainly, you can look up each issue, but this becomes tedious in practical circumstances. Having a solid foundation means that the practitioner already knows the answers to a lot of common questions.

The usability staff members need to be able to find answers to things they do not know. It is not acceptable for a usability person to simply make up recommendations out of thin air. There is a time to go find the right answer, and the practitioners need to be willing to check the research. They also have to know how to use the research. The usability field has research spread across about a hundred different sources, so the practitioner needs a library of articles and books they know well. They should also know how to find studies when needed.

The good usability practitioner regularly reads the literature to learn from new research studies. Sometimes he or she needs to retrieve studies to determine the best design decision. But unfortunately, understanding research papers is not easy. Research can provide invaluable insights, but it also has to be evaluated with great care. The usability practitioner must understand enough about experimental design and statistics to be able to interpret the research correctly. It is true that every staff member need not have this skill—a practitioner can ask for help. However, having this skill set within your organization is quite useful.

It is important to be familiar with a methodology so that the design process can be approached systematically. It is insightful to ask potential employees what to do to ensure that a Web site is usable. It is worrisome if they do not have a systematic methodology with clear activities and deliverables that build to a solution. Any activity like, "We will listen to the users" is suspect. What comes out of that listening? How does it really help the design? If they cannot talk their way through a systematic approach, practitioners are unlikely to follow a systematic approach, even if you hand them a copy of your methodology.

The development process requires a whole string of usability engineering activities. The usability practitioner must know how to do tasks like expert reviews, usability tests, contextual inquiries, task designs, wireframe designs, detailed designs, and functional specifications. Each of these tasks requires numerous subskills. For example, being able to "do" contextual inquiry includes the ability to stratify user segments, develop target user types, and develop a recruiting strategy. That is just one little part of the process. It is worthwhile to inventory the applicant's experience with these activities and ask some questions about his or her approach to specific tasks. However, because it is difficult to really get a sense for quality of work without direct experience, consider having potential employees work through a set of examples and evaluate the results of their work.

Being a usability engineer is not easy. As outlined here, a general usability practitioner needs to know a lot, but even more is required in addition to usability skills and knowledge. Usability engineers need to have a passion for making things usable. They need to have excellent communications skills, such as the ability to excel in team interaction, and a sense of charisma in evangelizing usability.

Education

While most usability practitioners have at least a master's degree in the field, there are some incredibly good people with a less formal educational background. But having a solid educational background is important. Many colleges and universities now offer usability programs. The Human Factors and Ergonomics Society Web site (www.hfes.org/) provides a listing of these courses. Currently, 62 programs listed for the United States include all kinds of usability work. The professors may specialize in, for example, factory workspaces, consumer products, the biomechanics of heavy lifting, or military equipment, so you have to look carefully to see which program actually provides appropriate skills for software design.

Senior usability people may have been in the field long enough to predate specific degree programs. Many of these people have master's or doctoral degrees in psychology instead of in human factors or usability.

A master's degree or more does not imply that the practitioner has a full set of skills. In fact, most programs typically provide basics, like how to read research and general design principles. Some courses may offer some experience in usability testing. However, keep in mind that education is really only the beginning of the process of becoming an expert practitioner. Experience is a critical factor and cannot be learned in the classroom.

Another validation that can be useful to consider is whether applicants are certified. There are several certification programs, as described in Chapter 6.

Experience

In looking at the applicants' experience, start with an assessment of the quality and range of their past work activities. There are limitations with people who have worked on just a single application and may have had a very limited role within that project, such as just running usability testing. Someone who has worked on a number of sites and applications has a wider perspective. Look for someone who has completed many different usability engineering activities, unless you are looking for someone with a limited scope. Even then, once someone is on board, he or she could easily be drafted to work on the development team for a critical project. It is therefore helpful if applicants have a wide spectrum of capabilities because, even though you may have hired them for a particular expertise like usability testing, it is likely you will need them to do other tasks as well.

It is also worthwhile to consider the quality of the project experience. While it is not that important that an applicant has worked on name-brand projects, it is important that he or she has worked on projects where usability was valued and given a significant role. Some usability practitioners spend years in a reactive mode—they basically sit in their offices and review designs, reacting to the aspects of the design that are so obviously awful that they can be seen without gathering data or completing a user-centered process. These people do not have much experience in supporting a solid process and appropriate methodology.

The usability field is still taught in the form of mentoring relationships. You can get a degree and read lots of books, but maturity of skills within this field really requires explicit mentoring. It is critically important to acquire staff members who have worked under a good mentor. Mentoring is perhaps the least organized aspect of the usability industry, yet it is also the most critical. There are many different aspects to work on: the common issues of team interaction, presentation style, and good writing, as well as the more important issues of design approach and specific usability engineering tasks. If you are not familiar with the specific mentors, it is hard to know if the potential employees have been well taught. It is a good idea to set up your own mentoring program, either in-house or with an outside consultant.

Usability Background That Includes Design

Usability work requires many analytical activities. The usability professional must be able to run studies, compile results, and make recommendations. There is research to be reviewed and assimilated, and valuable insights to be gained about user psychology and behavior. However, these activities are very different from the synthesis necessary for actual design. It is common to find skilled usability analysts who cannot design well. They may be familiar with the theory of design and be able to make contributions, but they will not be able to synthesize their knowledge to generate good interface designs.

In evaluating staff candidates, questions about design principles may evoke excellent theoretical responses from analytically oriented people who have no design capabilities. The individual may have worked on very successful design teams. However, others may have completed the actual design work within such teams. Therefore, it is essential to actually see each applicant do some design work and to evaluate the results.

There is a science to quality usability work—the research, methodology, and many hundreds of design principles. But there is also an intuitive side to design. The practitioner must pull together these insights in a "moment of magic." A huge disparity exists in candidates' abilities to do this. Ideally, the practitioner must be able to maintain a clear focus on the business goals and the overall context of the design. He or she must have a high-level model of the user's characteristics, limitations, and taskflow and must derive the interface so that it fits the shape of the user activities and needs. This is not to say that someone can do good design by pure intuition—process and science are needed. But there is indeed a step beyond the science. If you want usability staff members who are designers, look for the ability to take that intuitive step in synthesizing the results and creating the right solution.

Specialist vs. Generalist

You might find someone with a doctorate in usability who has a high standing academically, a long list of publications, and experience working in a large company with great success for many years. This person may be the world's expert in the psychological refractory period (the reaction time delay in stopping an action) as applied to handwriting errors. But this does not necessarily mean that he or she can do routine usability work. If handwriting is core to the business, this person may be a worthwhile specialist on the central usability team. But do not expect this person to be able to complete some of the more general usability activities, such as mentoring staff in development activities or developing quick tactical interface solutions under pressure.

Do not assume that specialized expertise in usability translates to general usability engineering skill or design skill. This may be the case, but more often it is not. So test carefully for both general skills and design skills.

Real Skills and Knowledge

This chapter has discussed the skills and knowledge essential for effective usability engineers. These essentials are not necessarily well known or agreed upon, however. Many people who consider themselves usability specialists do not have the skills and knowledge necessary to really undertake the work. Some people believe that if they have interviewed users one time before writing HTML code, they have done usability work. Some feel that if they have gotten feedback from users about their design, they are usability specialists. Others think they are experts because they have read books and even attended conferences. If you ask these people questions, they may even be able to provide a strong line of impressive responses. Their responses will include descriptions of the need for a user-centered perspective, how they "weave a tapestry of user experience," examples of data gathering with users, and perhaps a few terms from the latest magazine articles like "contextual inquiry" and "scenario." They may be very well intentioned and forward-looking, but they do not have the skills, knowledge, methods, tools, and resources to actually deliver on their promises. Put in a position of control, they will create flashy sites with unusual designs. They seem to be plausible candidates, but they will confuse and frustrate users. Their designs will be likely to fail, creating a big loss for your organization and your usability department. This lack of skills is often not evident until it is too late.

There are a few easy ways to detect this type of applicant. First, these candidates will rarely make any reference to research or be able to describe how to access studies in the field. Second, these people will usually not have a systematic methodology. They will talk in glowing terms of understanding users, but they will not have a process with clear activities and deliverables. Pay special attention to the lack of deliverables. Without concrete deliverables, it is very hard to determine whether the usability work is being done properly. Finally, there will probably be little discussion of concrete metrics. Good usability work is done to reach specific objectives. These results may take the form of a drop-off rate, efficiency, reduced training costs, and so on. Instead of describing the need for these kinds of results, this type of candidate will most likely offer flowery descriptions of a good user experience.

Interpersonal Skills and Level of Expertise

Usability specialists depend on good relationships with the development team. A specialist may have deep knowledge and a vast capacity for efficient design and good insights, as well as a thorough and systematic approach to his or her work. But without good interpersonal skills, the organization will actually receive little value.

It seems almost unfair: There are so many requirements for good usability specialists. They need knowledge of the literature, methodology, and design sense. Then, on top of this, they must work well with others in a team. Real challenges often arise related to the acceptance of new recruits by the team. If you bring in someone who is so high powered that he or she is way beyond the level of expertise of the other team members, the team may marginalize the person as a defense mechanism. No one wants to feel stupid, and having a really brilliant usability professional in a mediocre team makes the other team members feel inadequate. So what is the answer to this dilemma? The best solution is to ensure that you have a top-quality staff throughout your team.

However, in some cases you are staffing usability specialists for a team that is not world class. They may be building fairly routine applications. Their work may be less than mission critical. In this type of scenario, consider getting a good, solid usability professional who is perhaps not too advanced in skills beyond the other developers. Mismatch in expertise relative to the rest of the team can cause problems, and then those problems are blamed on poor interpersonal skills. Keep in mind that matching levels of expertise and good interpersonal skills are both important.

Archetypes

The four archetypes of usability workers were mentioned earlier in this chapter: the internal consultant, the documenter, the specialist, and the researcher. There is certainly a bit of each of these archetypes in every usability specialist. But the mix of these elements may be quite different. It makes sense to pick people who have a balance of the archetypes that will best fit with the job. For example, at HFI we look for people who are primarily general usability practitioners, though we are happy to have staff with a strong specialization in addition to their proclivity to practice. We need people with a little bit of the documenter in them because they need to create reports. In the same way, we avoid staff members who are researchers. Certainly, HFI does do research, and we have staff who enjoy this practice to some extent, but we avoid people who would do research for its own sake because this specialization does not match our needs.

When you are hiring, consider the mix of characteristics that will be helpful to your organization. You may primarily need general usability practitioners in the development teams, but in the central group, someone with documentation and research interests may be very useful. It is easy to discover the primary interests of applicants. Ask them what they enjoy most and hope to be doing in 5 years. Their focus will then become clear.

An Offshore Model

With all the challenges described throughout this chapter that may prevent organizations from locating and hiring high-quality usability staff, other options may need to be explored. Once the benefits of usability are understood, the spread of its use becomes viral. There is a rapid project-level increase in the desire to apply user-centered engineering practices. This increased interest puts unmanageable pressure on the (typically overcommitted) usability staff. This is the choke point: Once an understanding of the strategic impact of usability emerges, the internal usability staff typically cannot keep up with the demand for support. The model does not scale up easily.

This understaffing occurs because, as mentioned previously, well-trained usability specialists are difficult to find or very expensive. Ramping up the expert internal staff required to meet the increasing demand can be prohibitive. Consulting companies provide support for strained internal staff, but the cost of using consultant-based support for routine and sustained usability activities is also prohibitive. The need, however, is critical. Without sufficient staff to do the usability work, institutionalization will falter. Companies could continue to apply user-centered design principles to a small range of projects, but the lost opportunity cost of such a strategy is huge. Finding cost-effective usability staff offshore can provide a scalable solution.

The Challenges and Success Factors of Offshore Staffing

The communication challenges often experienced with an offshore model can be distilled to establishing an organizational structure that meets the four core requirements for project success when employing offshore resources:

1. Effectively managing the remote resources (both people and technology)
2. Ensuring an accurate and shared understanding of conventions, assumptions, and project goals
3. Maintaining quality of work standards
4. Delivering on schedule

Today's offshore models include components designed to help meet those requirements. Some elements relate directly to the specific development process and are explored in-depth in other chapters of this book.

- *A systematic, trackable methodology* ensures that projects proceed smoothly (Chapter 7).
- *Process-specific tools* reinforce correct use of the methodology (Chapter 8).
- *Technical certification* through training ensures an understanding of the methodology and tools (Chapter 6).

Factors unrelated to the specific development process are equally important.

- The *technical infrastructure* is secured with sufficient redundancy (e.g., backup generators).

- Bidirectional *cross-cultural education* is designed to address both day-to-day interactions and critical escalation paths.

Communication between local and remote team members is improved when the project team includes the following roles:

- A single *company-resident project contact point*
- An *offshore project team leader* sensitized to the native interaction styles

Communication between local and remote team members is not limited to interactions between these two individuals. However, they should be aware of all communications flowing back and forth between the various points of contact. This oversight ensures that collaboration is integrated and that the priorities and efforts of the remote team stay focused.

At HFI, we have been able to demonstrate that offshore teams can successfully complete all of the following usability engineering activities. (There are a few points where people need to travel to complete key tasks.)

- Expert reviews
- Usability testing (in person and remote)
- User interface structure design
- Standards development
- Prototype development
- Graphical treatment
- Detailed page design and layout
- Graphic library development
- Implementation/508-compliant[4] coding

Integrating a well-trained and well-managed remote usability team significantly increases the productivity of the organization as a whole. Furthermore, creating and training a remote usability team provides a cost-effective escape for the staffing chokehold.

---

4. "508" refers to Section 508 of the federal Rehabilitation Act. Section 508 mandates certain accessibility guidelines for federal agencies. For more information, visit www.section508.gov.

The Limits of Offshore Usability

Offshore teams work very well, but they cannot maintain the internal momentum for usability work. They can carry much of the development load, but they are not in a good position to be evangelists. There must be internal staff to maintain momentum and ensure that usability is not marginalized.

In addition, some mission-critical projects may need to be precisely tuned to the end user's perspective and culture. For these projects, the remote team may become part of a larger team, but a native usability specialist is important.

This chapter outlined a few of the roles important to the ongoing efforts of your central usability team and also provided strategies on what to look for when hiring staff. For organizations committed to making usability a routine part of the development cycle, a well-trained and managed remote team can provide the capacity to scale internal resources while establishing an institutionalized usability effort that is practical, successful, and cost-effective. The quality of your usability staff will play a big part in determining the success of your efforts and the reputation of your team. The next chapter provides specific information on strategies that will help you manage increasing usability demands across a variety of projects.

Chapter 13

Projects

> ➤ With a solid infrastructure and good staff, the usability work will be effective.
>
> ➤ All the project directors will want usability work, so you will quickly be short of usability staff.
>
> ➤ Prioritize projects by criticality (gold, silver, bronze, and tin).
>
> ➤ Put the best people on the high-priority projects and place new usability staff on less critical jobs.
>
> ➤ Use developers and others trained in usability to help, if necessary.
>
> ➤ For critical projects, get contract staff from usability consultancies.
>
> ➤ Use some top usability staff as consultants to help the newer staff (especially on higher-priority projects).
>
> ➤ Cut corners when planning usability work.
>
>   - Cut out functions.
>   - Focus usability work just on the critical modules (forget the administrative interface).
>   - Carefully scale back data gathering and usability testing.
>
> ➤ There are several ways to estimate your requirements for usability staff. Make an effort to get close to the required level, or the whole institutionalization effort may be wasted.

There is one sure sign of a successful institutionalization program: Lines-of-business managers will begin to routinely look for a user-centered process for their projects, and they will routinely look for usability practitioners to do the work. The result will be a severe shortage of usability staff. There is a natural tendency to react to the shortage of usability practitioners by spreading people thin and giving each practitioner many projects. However, this can cause their work to become less effective, and then people rightly wonder whether there is much value to this highly touted usability initiative. So resist the impulse to spread people thin. This chapter explores better ways to use the limited number of usability practitioners to good effect, with the assumption that your organization is unable to explore an offshore model similar to the one mentioned in the previous chapter.

Doing It Right

Assuming you have established the methodology, infrastructure, organization, and staffing and have engineered an acceptance of usability, it is now time to begin the routine application of usability engineering in your projects.

A mature usability process has many key hallmarks. Usability work starts very early in the development cycle, and there is no thought of having untrained technical staff develop a user interface and then test it, with the resulting frantic attempts to repair the flawed design. Instead, the usability process automatically starts as soon as the business need and strategy are identified. The usability practitioners—the leads on the project during the early stages—ensure that the strategy is refined and fully reflected in the actual site or application. The usability staff harmonizes the needs of the organization with the realities of user needs and limitations, creating a user interface structure that makes the navigation simple and straightforward.

Managing by Project Importance

Any site or application worth building is worth making usable, but there are differences in the criticality of usability work. An intranet facility that will be used by a few internal staff to maintain management accounting information is just not as critical, from a usability engineering viewpoint, as an e-commerce application that will be the company's sole channel for sales. Under the pressure of insufficient time and resources, it makes sense to do a bit of triage. You can assign a level to each project—gold, silver, bronze, or tin—and then give the most critical projects the highest level of usability engineering attention.

Gold   Give the most usability attention to projects that are mission critical to the company—projects that will make a big difference to the ongoing success of your organization. These gold projects must also have a lot riding on the user experience and performance. Usability may be important because there are many users, the users are hard to serve, or the performance stakes are very high—lives or large amounts of money might well be at stake.

Silver   It is likely that the bulk of your projects will be important but not wholly critical to the organization. These are usually not publicly sold applications or Web sites accessed by customers. They might be extranets used to access vendors or internal systems used to track and manage the work. For each high-profile public Web site operated by a company, there are probably ten supporting applications (ordering, shipping, inventory, and so on). While these are not examples of mission-critical usability, usability issues do matter. Usability may affect the ability of hundreds of users in the organization to perform efficiently; usability improvements can limit the need for training, reduce task time, and control errors. Many projects also have an impact on the company's vendors, such as widely used accounting and management information systems. These projects need serious usability support, but they are less critical than the gold projects.

Bronze   Many projects do not really need a major user-centered design process. They are simple facilities: perhaps an informational Web site with only a few users, where user experience and performance are not really in jeopardy. (A very simple site is harder to make incomprehensible then a complex site.) It is not worthwhile doing too much usability work on these projects, even when more resources are available in the future.

Tin   Usability practitioners should probably do no work at all on some projects. Occasionally, a project has almost no user interactions to worry about because it is entirely focused on internal database processing. Some "disaster" projects are poorly managed, have not had usability applied, and are in trouble. You can decide to intervene and try to save the project, or you can decide to let it go and not complete usability work on it because the chances are high that the project will be scrapped. In any case, on some projects it is a waste of resources to do any usability work.

Who Will Do the Usability Work?

Ideally, all the user-centered design activities can be completed by fully trained and experienced usability practitioners from the central team (in small companies) or by practitioners reporting to lines of business (in larger firms). However, there are alternatives. If the quality of work and timeliness cannot be allowed to suffer, consider using contract staff from usability vendors. This is the common solution for a gold project that has insufficient staff. These usability contractors may not know much about your organization, but they are experienced with design activities, can adhere to your specific customized standards, and should do a good job.

For silver projects, staff members who are not professional usability practitioners can complete the usability activities. It is possible for business analysts, systems analysts, programmers, and user representatives to do a credible job. This is not ideal, but it is a reasonable approach for silver projects. The usability of the site or application is likely to suffer to some degree, but you can take measures to minimize the problem.

If other staff members are standing in for usability practitioners, they should have usability training. Without training, the progress will be slow, and the work will likely be of poor quality. This training can and should be in the form of both classroom training and on-the-job training. Individuals with more experience and training can act as guides or mentors for newer individuals as they work on projects. This ensures that the work does not go too far off the path. Even a few days of mentoring from an experienced consultant can keep well-intentioned teams from expensive detours.

For bronze and tin projects, less usability investment is justified. You might have the project staff members take a few days of training in usability design, but you are unlikely to provide much consultative support. The developers must then make do with their training and the company infrastructure they can access.

Different Strategies for Practitioner Involvement

Some companies seem to feel that the best way to deploy usability practitioners is to have them work as part of a development team that designs by committee. If this is the corporate design process, it does help to have a usability professional in the mix, but for significant development efforts, design of the user interface by committee is fiercely inefficient. Usability work is best done in cycles of data gathering and quiet work. It is important that the usability work involve others (e.g., developers, graphic designers, and so on), but for significant development efforts, the usability practitioner must be able to complete design work outside of committees. The practitioners need to study the users and find out how they react, then digest these insights and make design changes individually or in a very small group. It is painful to see committees discuss the wording of some link for a full hour. With 15 people working, that link costs 15 person-hours to draft! It is fine to have a committee participate in a walkthrough, but it is a poor way to do design, even if there are plenty of usability practitioners available.

When working on a silver or bronze project with limited resources, the usability staff can take an evaluative role. This means that the project team creates designs, and the usability staff reviews the work and provides feedback. The project team takes the feedback, makes changes to the designs, and returns the designs for another usability review if necessary. This process is actually less than ideal: It involves risks, and it may be inefficient. For example, if the data gathering with users is poorly done, staff might work hard on unneeded or incorrectly structured screens. A lot of review cycles may be needed to reach a good design. This can be frustrating and even a bit adversarial. (In time the developers will flinch just seeing the usability staff.) While this is not an ideal strategy, it does use less of the usability engineer's time. You can support an entire project with just a few days of help from a practitioner. You can consider this approach, therefore, for a silver or bronze project, but not for a gold project.

For silver and some lower-end gold projects, there is an alternative that often has great success: The usability practitioners take full control and responsibility for the development of the user interface structure only. This means that the usability practitioners are not designing every page or screen but are creating only the critical structure. To accomplish this, they may have to review or test the original application or site. The practitioners use data gathered from users to structure a site that is practical, simple, and efficient to navigate. The practitioners then test this design to ensure that it is self-evident and that the graphic treatment gives an impression that supports the brand values of the organization. Then the design can be given to people with basic training (e.g., business analysts) who can use the standards to proliferate the detailed pages needed under the structural design. The usability staff can provide coaching and review the detailed designs created by the developers. This puts the scarce usability practitioners on the most critical work. Remember that 80% of usability is determined by the structural design.[1] Therefore, if the structure is right, not too much can go seriously wrong in the detailed design. This is particularly true if the work is done under standards. The detailed design requires less demanding work

---

1. This figure is based on HFI's 20 years of experience with hundreds of clients, across thousands of user-centered design projects.

(which often takes 80% of the time), and it can be completed by staff members who are less scarce and might actually be more familiar with the detailed requirements than the new usability practitioners.

For high-end gold projects, there is no alternative but to employ skilled usability practitioners. They must certainly do the structural design work, and it is also advisable to have them complete, or at least lead, the detailed screen design and usability testing. This yields the best-quality designs in the shortest time.

Working Smart

When the lack of usability practitioners is acute, a number of strategies can help. While it is easy to get frightened by the magnitude of the problem and frantically try to do everything at once, this is the time to get organized and plan carefully. Staying up late on the project just makes you inefficient; you will have to fix all the fatigue-induced errors in addition to the onslaught of new work. Instead of panicking and working late nights, work smart.

- *Trim unnecessary functions.* Usability practitioners can often identify functions that are not needed at all or are at least secondary. It is often possible to trim the size of the deliverable and still end up with a useful offering. In fact, many projects benefit from this trimming of excess features.

- *Focus the usability work on the important modules of the interface.* You can apply the same triage principles discussed earlier for projects to the modules of an application, rating them gold, silver, bronze, or tin. For example, you might find that the product display and checkout pages are gold, but there are a whole set of administrative screens that will be seen only by a few highly trained and motivated internal systems administrators, so you can rate the administrative module bronze and not worry too much about it. You can use the same schemes within the project as suggested for whole projects. So, a systems analyst might design the administrative module, with a review by a usability practitioner. Otherwise, the usability practitioner is busy perfecting the checkout process that is essential to the project's success.

- *Use an effective but scaled-back usability testing strategy.* For example, it is not desirable to eliminate the data gathering and testing early in the process because they are very important and relatively inexpensive. However, you might be able to test fewer participants or test in fewer locations. If pressed, you could eliminate the final usability testing. This test is expensive and tends to only fine-tune the design.

- *Consider using remote testing.* Being face-to-face with users during data gathering offers much value. The nuances of facial expressions can give good usability specialists important insights into directions of inquiry. But remote testing is becoming a viable alternative: Remote testing techniques are improving, and technologies are being developed quickly for the use of remote video. For simple tests, you may be able to cut the time required by using remote testing methods. For example, sometimes you can just send an image or questionnaire to the participants and then talk to them by phone.

- *Consider the possibility of sharing testing sessions between projects.* If more than one project is targeted at a given user population, it may be possible to test both projects at once. The main cost of a data gathering or usability test is getting the participants in the room, so extending a test session from an hour to 90 minutes may let you get data to support two programs from the single session.

- *Scale back the number of participants in studies and the number of different geographies tested.* You can get some pretty good usability testing data from a dozen people. Testing in lots of different regions of the United States, for example, often yields few new insights. These are reasonable ways to scale back. But do not scale back by using internal staff members as stand-ins for actual users in data gathering and testing. Internal staff members are almost always different from typical users, and their input can lead you astray. It is also ill advised to reduce the number of participants to less then a dozen; it is too easy to be overly influenced by an unusual person who just happens to show up in a small study. You'll also know there's a problem when you encounter the same problems repeatedly.

- *Have a single practitioner work on a number of different projects.* This can be a great way to stretch your scarce usability resources. However, remember that this is quite challenging, and not all practitioners can juggle projects well. If you are going to have one person work on many projects, he or she will need to work in a guidance/advice role only.

Efficient Project Planning

There is much that can be done in the project planning stage to make the work faster and more efficient.

- *Use standard project planning techniques to track phases and activities.*
- *Watch for cases where a critical path can put the whole schedule in jeopardy.* For example, when working on an interface structure, the day that the project is approved, start working out the details of participant acquisition for the data gathering sessions. The data gathering is the third or fourth activity, but getting participants lined up can take weeks. If not started immediately, this could delay the whole project.
- *Work concurrently.* Usability work often allows for concurrent activities. Graphic artists can be working on designs while the usability practitioners are writing questionnaires. Results can be tabulated for the first day of testing while the second day of testing is in progress.
- *Be ready to make adjustments.* Usability work is often influenced by outside factors, such as developer activities and business needs. Be prepared to review your project, plan often, and make adjustments.
- *Hold firm.* People tend to think that usability is the area to change or cut back when time is limited. Don't let others force you into agreeing to do a task in less time than it will take.

Organizational Support for Usability

By Dana Griffith, CUA, Web Consultant—Interactive Media, American Electric Power

The people at the highest level in my group believe in usability. For them, it has become part of the process of creating a new site or revising a site, so we probably have a little different approach to the question of institutionalizing usability. Because we manage the corporate Web site and the company intranet, we are able to address usability at the point when design decisions are being made, without holding up the project for any measurable length of time.

Estimating Usability Work

As you plan and manage the flow of projects given a limited set of usability practitioners, it helps to accurately estimate the requirements for different projects. This allows better allocation of the resources available and can also provide a good estimate of the number of usability staff members you will eventually need within your organization.

For gold and silver projects, you can usually get a good idea of the level of effort needed for usability work by gauging a percentage of the overall project effort. Very small projects end up with large percentages of usability work because there is a limit on the amount you can reduce the interface development effort. No matter how simple the project, for gold and silver projects, you need to access data from users and test the design concepts. This said, you are likely to see a maximum of perhaps 25% of the project effort spent on usability. With larger projects, say, a typical e-commerce site costing $3 million, you might spend 10% of the budget on usability. As projects get larger, there may be a further reduction down to about 7% as you gain the ability to take advantage of economies of scale. If your plan for a gold or silver project has less than 5% of the budget allocated for usability work, you are probably making a mistake.[2]

Table 13-1: *Estimated Time Frame for Usability Activities*

Activity	Elapsed Time	Usability Practitioner Person-Days
Usability test of the current design	3 weeks	12–20 days
Expert review	2 weeks	10–20 days
User interface page design	6–10 weeks	45–65 days
Draft detailed page design	1 day per page (very roughly)	1 day per page
Quick formative usability tests	4 days	4 days
Final usability test before release (one country)	2–5 weeks	10–40 days
Final usability test before release (five different languages and countries)	4–7 weeks	30–60 days

You can also make estimates based on the type of usability work being completed, as shown in Table 13-1. This approach is more accurate than taking a simple percentage, but it is still an estimate; your results may vary. For example, an inexperienced team may take a much longer time than a seasoned one. Other factors can influence these typical estimates widely, such as the complexity of the application or product, the number of different users, and the need to develop a product for use across different languages or cultures.

The efforts you have made to build an effective infrastructure with high-quality staff are sure to lead you to a certain amount of success. However, it remains important to manage your projects carefully. By following the tips and strategies in this chapter, you should be able to maintain a good level of momentum. The next chapter elaborates on some of the ongoing activities and responsibilities of the established usability group.

---

2. The figures in this paragraph are based on HFI's experience with its customer base. In addition, the 10% figure is also cited in a report by Nielsen and Gilutz [2003].

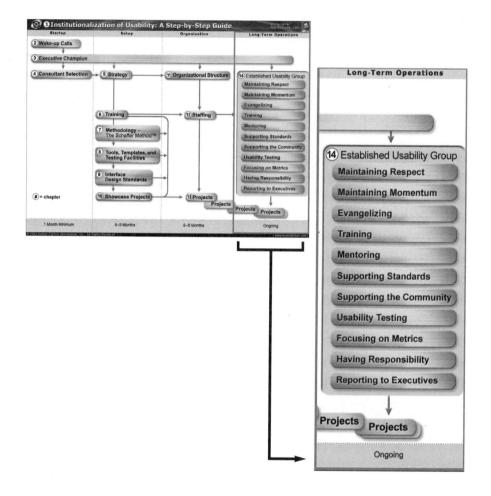

Part IV

Long-Term Operations

In the Long-Term Operations phase, the full infrastructure and the usability team become operational. Usability is now a routine part of every project.

- You will no longer build a site or application first and then merely hope it really will be what users need.
- You will not let the technical design of a system alone drive the selection of controls for ease of use.
- You will be ahead of your competitors if they have not completed their own usability efforts—this is a significant benefit to your brand and corporate efficiency.

The organization is working effectively, but there must be an ongoing process of renewal, evaluation, and enhancement. Usability is not such a simple issue that the organization will continue to flourish without attention from the executive level and ongoing excellence from within the usability team.

Chapter 14

Activities of the Established Usability Group

➤ The central group is responsible for the overall usability initiative in the organization. Keep usability vibrant, effective, and respected.

- Don't be marginalized, ignored, or diverted back to a technology focus.

- Maintain momentum by planning the work for excitement and visible progress.

- Evangelize usability by constantly hosting events to share the lessons learned and convey excitement about the value of usability.

- Train the new people to keep the knowledge of user-centered design in your organization. Also, enhance and update the skill sets of existing staff.

- Mentor the usability staff working for the project teams.

- Update the design standard and provide consultation to help developers follow the rules.

- Form a community of interest. Support formal activities, such as information sharing sessions, that provide mutual emotional support.

- Conduct usability tests objectively, as outsiders to the project team.
- Measure usability to show your investment is working and highlight areas for improvement.
- Take responsibility for usability throughout the organization.
- Report your progress and achievements to executives.

Once you get the infrastructure in place and the organization built, the usability group has to maintain and grow the usability process, continuously reinforce the value of usability, and integrate the user-centered methodology. While working on projects, the usability practitioners follow the methodology, use the best research and principles available at the time, call internal consultants and specialists from the central usability team for support, and occasionally demonstrate and report the success of a user-centered perspective.

The executive responsible for the central group may provide resources and encouragement and may clear obstacles from the pathway to growth, but the heavy lifting of the continued usability process is completed by the central team. This chapter focuses on the most important activities the central usability team can perform to keep the usability institutionalization current and vibrant.

Maintaining Respect and Negotiating Effectively

Usability practitioners face some resistance on an ongoing basis—it is the nature of the development process. The usability community needs to maintain enough respect so that it can get the users' needs fulfilled without being marginalized, ignored, or overrun with technology taking precedence over usability.

For example, a usability designer may tell a developer that users need a display that collects all their data in one place. The developer quickly sees that this is hard to support: It will be necessary to link calls to a number of databases, and greater processing power will be needed. The developer naturally wonders whether this usability practitioner knows what is going on. Is this really going to make a difference to the user? Will it make a difference to the business?

First, the usability practitioner and the developer need to try to negotiate a mutually agreeable solution based on a shared under-standing of the user issues and technical constraints. If they can't reach an agreement, a consultant from the central group needs to review the conflict and quickly decide whether, in fact, the user needs are critical. If they are not, the central team needs to admit the reality and negotiate something different. It is acceptable if the cen-tral team occasionally corrects a recommendation from a usability practitioner on a project team. Once reviewed and confirmed by the central team, the recommendation must be supported with examples from the literature or research studies demonstrating the effect. Usually, it takes only a few such studies to earn a reputation of hav-ing research-based recommendations. Achieving this reputation means that eventually not all decisions will have to be defended. But occasionally throughout the organization, the usability practi-tioners will need to step in and push the user's perspective against coding convenience.

A special concern is the ability of the usability practitioners to man-age claims about technical feasibility. In one common dynamic, developers claim that a recommendation is infeasible when it is in fact feasible. The usability practitioner needs enough technical savvy to understand both sides of the interface. It must become a habit for usability staff to dig deeper into claims of infeasibility. For example, what does "That will take too long" really mean? Does it refer to coding time, response time, or something else?

Sometimes the technical staff members attempt to overpower a less experienced usability practitioner. Again, this is a time when central usability consultants must step in. They must know enough about the technology to be able to assess the situation. The usability practi-tioner might need a course in technical limitations so he or she will make fewer infeasible recommendations in the future. More often, the technical staff members need to be shown that "technobabble"

The Value of a Research-Based Approach to Usability

By Janice Nall, Chief, Communication Technologies Branch, National Cancer Institute

At the National Cancer Institute (NCI), we needed a research-based way to make decisions about the way we design Web sites.

We developed research-based guidelines, and that was the turning point. With guidelines in place, it's not a manager saying what to do, and it's not the head of the Institute saying it. It's the users saying it, and it's the research—the literature. In our culture, that's what it's all about. So it's making what we do work within the culture here that's important.

I think the guidelines have given us a much more powerful voice than we expected originally. We developed them from a research-based approach because we thought it was the right way to do it. We truly underestimated the power of having the data and having the user's voice represented. Very few people aren't willing to make changes based on the evidence-based guidelines.

The largest amount of hard-core resistance we see tends to come from programmers and some graphic designers. That's why we try to get them to attend training or observe testing. If we sense any resistance to usability from developers or designers, we test the current site or some other site and force them into the observation room so they can see people struggling, and it helps them understand the process. We try to do it in a very nonthreatening way so that they're part of the team helping us try to make it better.

will not be accepted as a substitute for the hard work needed to meet the user's needs.

Maintaining respect is important for the competitive health of the organization. Organizations that marginalize the usability practitioners

Roadblocks in the Path to Good Usability— The IT Department

By Harley Manning, Research Director, Forrester Research

A big impediment to getting better Web sites is the struggle over implementation with the IT department. Who said that the average IT staffer knows or cares about usability? The fact of the matter is, if you're in IT, you know three or four different programming languages and maybe have a good grasp of systems architecture—even the most opaque user interface looks easy to you.

So the IT folks are not exactly your typical business user, nor are they necessarily sympathetic to your typical business user. And they're not typically evaluated on how well they deliver usable software, either. They are—to steal a phrase—"the inmates running the asylum" [Cooper 1999]. They have different goals and different things they're trying to optimize.

We just did a survey in this area, and you know what? The number one consideration for IT managers buying enterprise software was whether or not it was compatible with the rest of their architecture. Usability was near the bottom of their decision criteria.

You are not going to have good usability if you don't co-opt IT because you need to make sure that what was coded matches the original design. And as we all know, a lot of times you send your prototype off to be coded, and it comes out working differently and looking differently than what you sent in.

And that leads you inevitably back to the top of the organization. Because who is the common manager of IT, marketing, and the design group (if one exists)? It's someone with a title like COO or CEO.

One change that has to happen to make usability part of the culture is to get your IT act together. You have to have a repeatable and reliable IT process. Otherwise, even if you design a great product, it won't materialize.

in favor of coding ease eventually get nasty wake-up calls. Keep the level of respect for usability high, and there will be no such recurring wake-up calls.

Maintaining Momentum

It is critical to keep momentum at a rate that is motivating for the usability staff and development team. The usability effort does not need to be too aggressive. Companies that mandate usability and try to implement it instantly do not do well. It takes time to disseminate usability into the organization, but there must be forward movement.

One trick is to initially keep the effort focused on smaller projects. Even if resources are limited, you can make one or two projects into showcases. In this way, even a small commitment is visible and motivating. After allowing time for percolation, you can start to tackle larger projects. Make sure you don't have a few practitioners trying to work on too many projects. If you have a small amount of staff applied to a huge organization, your efforts will be invisible, and you will lose momentum.

Evangelizing

The central usability group must provide information and share the lessons learned on the value of usability. This means making presentations on a regular basis. These presentations can share project examples, new research findings, and progress in the metrics of usability. Beyond formal presentations, it is necessary to implement a constant process of communication with individuals and small groups, including quiet lunches and personal opportunities in social gatherings. Usability practitioners need to exploit every possible venue for communication and sharing. Most importantly, the team members need to convey their excitement about and commitment to the usability effort: They need to evangelize!

When missionaries travel to new countries, they translate their beliefs into the local language. They translate their ideas and value systems so they fit with the local traditions and needs. In a similar manner, the usability evangelist must talk the business language of the organization and translate the value of usability so it meets the objectives of the development teams and other groups. It is great to share some of the jargon of usability, but especially in the beginning of the institutionalization process, it is best to incorporate the knowledge of usability into the local language. If you are talking to business people, talk

The Role of the Central Usability Team
By Arnie Lund, Director of Design and Usability, Microsoft

My design and usability team should be a place where we learn and build our intellectual capital around good design. It should be where we abstract from the many projects we're doing those lessons and insights that cut across releases and products. The resulting intellectual capital should make us more and more effective over time, and I would hope that eventually what we learn would work its way outside of Microsoft and into the broader user experience field.

One goal we have in Microsoft is to build community across the corporation and then advance the community. As Microsoft design and usability managers, we are creating a long-term plan for the company about where the user experience practice within Microsoft should be heading. The plan is based on a view of where the company is going, how technology is evolving, a sense of emerging user experience methods and tools, and what that means for a vision of design and usability five years out. We are trying to figure out where we need to be to maximize our contribution to the business and to our customers in that time frame. We will then draw out the implications for career growth, for skills growth, for new tools that we need

(continued)

The Role of the Central Usability Team *(cont.)*

to develop, for design and usability, for techniques and methods, for hiring, for internal training—indeed, all the things we believe we will need to do to advance the community and practice of design and usability within Microsoft.

As I think about promoting an understanding of the importance of design and usability within Microsoft, I think about what we do already and what we can do in the future. There is a corporate newsletter, of course, where stories about product successes and individual usability group case studies appear. I think we can leverage that more. Design and usability is built into the corporate training that all new employees go through, into individual internal courses, and into corporate events. We had a Design Day a couple of months ago that a lot of managers attended (along with the design and usability communities). Several of us spoke, there were panels, and there were booths. We were able to play an educational role and network in ways that helped grow our impact. There are many opportunities to do the PR that opens doors.

One of the results of the focus on personas within Microsoft is that the personas get turned into posters that get mounted on walls. They direct people's attention to the users and heighten awareness of the research behind the personas. Here in our organization we are talking about creating design walls and user experience walls to surround the project teams with information about the users and the emerging designs. It keeps them focused on the users and what we do; and it engages them in where we are going and how we are thinking about it. It invites their input. We always try to get people involved in lab testing. We have even been taking advantage of the ability to stream the video from the testing over the intranet so product teams can participate from their desks without having to travel to the lab. The goal is to get as many people on the teams as possible engaged in the user-centered design process.

about conversion rates and call time. It's advisable not to use usability jargon exclusively, including terminology like "target acquisition," "scenarios," and "function allocation." The usability evangelist needs to have the ability to translate these concepts into familiar terms.

It is hard to estimate the time required to evangelize. It is closer to a lifestyle than a specific task, but certainly there are presentations to prepare and meetings to organize. The concrete parts of the evangelization role probably add up to a half- or full-time position in a large organization. The manager of the usability team often assumes much of this responsibility.

Evangelists must have a certain charisma that equates to a burning desire to share their knowledge. Evangelists must communicate a certain excitement and must show how their insights can directly transform the listener's life. The commitment of an evangelist is contagious and necessary; if the staff members of the central group become complacent and bored, the whole effort will likely flounder.

Training

During the initial phases of your institutionalization program, a series of training classes probably brought people up to speed and conveyed essential skills. This training was necessary, but for a competitive organization, training is never completely finished. There must be an ongoing training program, and the internal usability team should take charge of this effort. However, the team may not need to be responsible for all the training—in most organizations it doesn't make sense to maintain the more complex and less often used courseware, and there are not enough presentations of most usability training classes to keep the trainers fully occupied. Despite this reality, the central group must have responsibility for the training program as a whole.

Usability training should be a part of the orientation of new staff. Otherwise, the benefit of a user-centered perspective may be slowly diluted by new staff members who don't receive the usability orientation. In addition to the basic orientation, some new members need to learn specific skills to work on particular types of projects or particular usability activities. For example, you may need someone to specialize in wireless devices or usability testing. Over time, your ongoing skills training will probably need to cover the full range of usability engineering capabilities as new staff members appear.

The usability effort should also include ongoing presentations of the training used for the initial orientation to usability, including skills training, training on standards, training on the usability engineering insights specific to the organization's domain, and training on new and special topics.

Existing usability staff members also need continuous training and professional development. The people in the central group may benefit from attending technical conventions, where they can learn about new research or methods and talk with colleagues in other industries to share problems and pick up tips. Usability staff can also benefit from taking advanced courses. These courses may include such topics as research updates and new usability methodologies (e.g., remote testing).

It is clearly motivating for the team members to see that the process is working. It is also motivating if they have a growing set of credentials showing their competency. Many benefits occur when staff members gain advanced degrees and certifications: Coworkers in other groups develop more respect for the usability team, the field stays new and interesting to the usability staff members, and their skill sets increase. It is also a confidence builder—even certificates of completion can build confidence.

Mentoring

The usability staff members working on the project teams have a "dotted line" relationship with the central group. This means that the central group cares about them and is there to advocate for them in politics and policy and to help handle problems. But most directly, the central group should be there to mentor the usability staff on the project teams. Depending on the corporate culture, this might be either a very formal process or an informal one.

The mentoring job is challenging because there is no single path of mentoring needed. Some staff members need insights into data gathering methods, some need to build confidence so they can run their first solo usability test, and others need help interacting with developers.

Mentoring may be only one part of a person's job and should require a different perspective than working on projects. The mentor should attend to the growth of the usability practitioner, rather than worrying about meeting deadlines and ensuring the efficacy of design on a project too.

Supporting Standards

In the Setup phase of institutionalization, you created a set of methodological standards and interface design standards. Developing these standards required a big investment, but they will not endure or be used unless they are supported in several ways.

The standards are living documents. New and improved procedures will be added to the methodology, and new page types and additional rules will be added to the design standards. The usability team must constantly monitor the design process and find opportunities for improvement. Innovations rarely come from a theoretical analysis of the existing standards; they come from watching the direct contact between the standards and the design work. Necessity spawns inventions, and the usability team has to gather these inventions and add them to the standards.

The time required to collect new methods and place them into the standards varies based on the complexity of the design challenges. It also varies depending on the process required for getting consensus and approval for changes. At HFI, for example, we have four cycles of upgrades to our methods and templates each year. The GUI standards require fewer changes by now, but the browser standards are still growing. The time taken for collecting enhancements and facilitating the approval process might be a half-time job.

There is little value in having a methodology or a design standard if there is no one to go to with questions. No document is so thorough that there will not be issues about the design decisions. There are special needs based on users, taskflows, environments, technologies, and

---

Advocating Usability through a Strong Sense of Community

By Feliça Selenko, Principal Technical Staff Member, AT&T

I think one of the most important ways to share an understanding of usability is to do it one person/one project at a time. Usability experts need to take the time to look for and take advantage of every opportunity to advocate usability, its bottom-line cost benefits, and the respective user performance research. They need to have their "soapbox" and a usability road show ready to go at all times, in order to support any and all requests for information about usability and its benefits. This creates a strong network of supporters and "prophets" to help spread the word.

Colleagues have said that my enthusiasm and consistent commitment throughout the years have kept the team going through any hard times experienced by the telecommunications industry. The words that come to mind that create a sense of community are enthusiasm, camaraderie, empathy, dedication, sincere support, responsiveness, optimism, and fun—really believing in the value of the usability discipline and treasuring the community we have. Logistically, we have a grassroots, committed, cross-organizational team that meets monthly on a two-hour conference call. We discuss everything: project dilemmas, rumors, industry articles/conferences, organizational issues, usability tools, and standards, as well as personal changes and triumphs. By keeping it practical, focused, and fun, we all look forward to maintaining our connection.

business strategies. Sometimes the design teams need someone to talk to—someone with wider experience and the ability to give definitive guidance on methods and design. The team members need a consultant—and they can talk to one on the central usability team.

It is important to have consistent guidance from the central group regarding standards issues. This is not a call for rigidity because standards need to be interpreted in each context, but there must still be coherence to the answers that teams get from their standards consultants. Therefore, it is best to charge just one or two people with this task. If there are two, they should work closely together. However, for most organizations, a single person can answer standards questions, and in smaller organizations, this might be half of one person's responsibilities.

In addition, the tools need to be supported. This may include getting the best software and usability testing equipment to be used in the methodology, or it may mean working with systems staff to select content management systems and other productivity-enhancing applications to ensure that the usability design process is supported. This can be a half- to full-time job in most organizations.

Supporting the Community

Usability staff members often quickly form a community of interest within their company. They may not be formally connected within the organization, but they have traditionally banded together. In the past, the usability team often consisted of a small group of people who were undervalued and often under attack. Developers saw them as an annoyance and tried to marginalize them because they were seen as working in a "soft" and unimportant area. Generally, a persecuted minority clings together, and the usability staff members were no exception. Their mutual support was often all that sustained the effort, providing a conduit of information and resources, as well as mutual emotional support. Alone yet surrounded by people with a system-centered view, it was easy to start thinking you were crazy and to lose the will to keep working. But the small circle of colleagues made all the difference.

In the future, we will not be able to rely on the "small surrounded group" phenomenon to maintain a lively usability engineering community. Usability will be accepted and routine. Therefore, we will need to work explicitly to keep a lively community going.

A community of usability professionals gains strength by working on projects together. These projects may include standards, tools, or collective presentations to management. The simple act of working together forms relationships, increases group cohesiveness, helps motivate the institutionalization effort, and increases the transfer of information and support.

A powerful method is the project-sharing presentation. Periodically, the usability specialists can share with each other presentations to recount the best insights and breakthroughs from their projects. Each project team has only a short time, perhaps 15 minutes, to present, so these aren't long-winded process discussions or explanations of the whole project. They can just share the major insights and innovations. Teams can go beyond presentations and provide skits and interactive demonstrations. In addition, it is helpful when teams show concrete before/after examples, which provide a quick and powerful way to share lessons learned among all the usability staff.

Performing Usability Testing

It is quite possible to have the usability practitioners on project teams do all of their own usability testing. However, there are two reasons to have some of the testing done by the central group. The first reason is the ability to economize. It is simple to hire specialists to do usability testing. You can maintain a small pool of usability testing staff members who do not have the capability to complete all the activities in user-centered design but are knowledgeable about running tests.

The second reason is objectivity. Some usability practitioners have trouble accepting that users can find lots of problems with designs, but that does not mean these practitioners are bad designers. These types of practitioners often feel resistant, and some will even argue with usability testing subjects to try to convince them that the design makes sense. Once, I watched a developer try to explain to a participant the difference between the OK and Apply buttons. With enough explanation, the participant seemed to agree that there was a difference (or more likely, he was bored by the discussion and just wanted to move on). In these cases, it helps to have someone else run the test.

Focusing on Metrics

A common management principle advises, "If you can't measure it, you can't manage it." By measuring usability you can know that your investment is working. You can tell what areas need more work and can improve your process. The central usability team needs to create and maintain the usability metrics that make sense to your business.

One type of metric describes the process of user-centered design. It is good to track the number of staff hired and trained, the number of people working on usability issues, and the number of projects that do or do not apply the user-centered methodology. The main purpose of these metrics is to validate that usability work is actually being done and to show the growth and stability of usability in the organization. Note that this is basically cost accounting. Although you may be happy to see a solid investment in usability, this does not actually measure anything valuable for the organization. While you will have an indication of cost in hand, there had better be a solid improvement in the business results to justify this expenditure.

It is helpful to have periodic empirical demonstrations of the value of usability work. These focused studies generally look at a very specific before/after design scenario. For example, the site may have a point of high drop-off. If usability work can reduce the drop-off, you may be able to attribute significant improvement in sales to that change. If specific functions in an application can be improved, those improvements can be measured and reported.

One thing to watch for is being satisfied with hearing that "the users liked it." This kind of anecdotal feedback is better than nothing and certainly better than being told the users have created their own paper system as an alternative to your design. However, it is far better to have specific data and to hear that a survey shows a specific movement in the rating for the site or application. It would be even more compelling to find that the time needed to complete a checkout process has dropped by 25%. But the most compelling information is directly tied to the business needs—how much money the usability effort makes, how much money it saves, and the specific amount of increase in customer satisfaction.

If you do not know where you have been, it is hard to demonstrate progress. A summative usability test at the end of the design process reporting that applications for insurance are completed in 2.5 minutes is a bit hard to interpret. It seems like a reasonable time, but is it an improvement? This is the reason you need benchmark testing. In a benchmark test, participants complete a set of representative tasks, and usability staff measure time, error rate, and subjective ratings. A similar group of participants completes the same testing with the same tasks every 6 or 12 months. Then you can see whether the changes you have been making have affected the user experience or performance. This also allows you to benchmark the time required for expert users to complete the representative tasks. This combination gives a very good indication of progress.

Many metrics look at user performance and subjective reports from customers. These kinds of metrics are interesting, but they can be misleading. For example, Jared Spool, Founding Principal of User Interface Engineering, had the following insights to share regarding privacy and the Internet, demonstrating that you cannot rely only on what users say:

> In April of 2002, Princeton Survey Research Associates surveyed 1,000 adult Internet users about their concerns with privacy on the Internet. In the survey, only 18% said they never read privacy policies when shopping online; 57% said they check the privacy policy most of the time, or every time they shop.

Yet, in our study of more than 1,000 shopping sessions, where we actually observed what users did while shopping, we noticed that only two users ever checked the site's privacy policy. And for those two users, it had no effect on their shopping behavior. This is yet one more case of users doing something different from what they say they do.[1]

Different business models require different objectives to measure the metrics directly connected to the success of the site or application. This could be a sale of an application, the conversion of site visitors, the size and breadth of shopping basket cross-sell volume, average call-handling time, or qualified leads generated and the resulting sales. There are potentially hundreds of useful metrics. However, in the end they need to be tied firmly to business results. For example, while it might be encouraging that 92% of customers respond on a questionnaire that they would purchase on a Web site, it is much more meaningful to see how many actually make a purchase.

Having Responsibility

The central usability group takes responsibility for usability throughout the organization. This responsibility includes an attitude of involvement and concern, as well as a set of specific activities. The central group should watch for projects that need usability help and areas of the company business that will benefit from usability work. The central group needs to make sure that the projects get the attention they need.

Ensuring that usability practitioners are working on important projects is the primary requirement. After assigning a practitioner to a project, the organization must provide the necessary skills, methodology, standards, tools, and channels of communication. The central group has to constantly review the internal process and consider the lessons learned and opportunities uncovered.

---

1. From a letter to Human Factors International, September 2003. Reproduced with permission.

It is hard to quantify the time it takes to do this type of management work. In a sense, it takes little extra time because much of the work occurs in the context of other activities. For example, a central group consultant reviewing a voice response system might hear about issues on a new project or might find a new menu type like Skip and Scan that can apply to all voice systems throughout the organization. If this new menu reduces drop-through to a human operator by 5%, the savings may be modest for a single small application, but the value is vastly multiplied if applied throughout the organization. Only a central usability team is likely to be a good conduit for such insights.

Reporting to Executives

Usability is one of those challenging and valuable initiatives that does not happen on its own. There are many different parts of the initiative, and few are elements you can afford to forget. You must address complex issues of change management and acceptance. Management will eventually understand that usability metrics are as critical to the business as gross sales and support costs. In addition to ensuring that usability is taking place within the company, the central usability team must maintain a usability presence within the executive suite.

The executive champion helps deliver this message, but its real content comes from the central group. The members should have the examples that demonstrate how usability makes a difference and the metrics to prove it. The group must understand the champion's strategic perspective and move forward on that track, improving the process and ensuring continuation.

Some of the central group's attention must always be focused on the executive champion and the other key executives in the organization. The amount of time required varies depending on the dispersion of the executive team. A closely knit team all in one location is easy to manage. With the key people properly briefed, there is little more to do. In this situation, it takes only a few days of effort each month. With a more complex executive team, it can be nearly a half-time job keeping everyone appraised on the progress, value, and needs of the usability effort.

My Nine Principles to Keep Institutionalization Motivated

By Colin Hynes, Director of Site Usability, Staples

1. *Go deep first and that will help you go wide later.* Get the solid gains first and don't try to sell yourself too thin. If you work on ten different projects with three usability experts, you won't do any of them well. Then you'll just be perceived as a veneer on the process instead of having real impact. When we started this group, I knew we needed to get some solid wins in a very deep and effectual way. We did that, and then we went on to other projects that helped us spread our influence as we built the group.

2. *Quantify gains made from projects* that were led or deeply impacted by usability and translate that into ROI [return on investment]. We have held up the improvements that usability made to the Staples.com registration process as one of our hallmark projects. We improved the drop-off rate—the percentage of users leaving our site—in that area by 72%. As I speak about the usability group, I constantly reference that number and say, "Look what happens when you include usability and then tie that back to numbers." The business folks listen when they see these types of gains.

3. *Create a selling document* with video clips and numbers that resonates with budget owners. I spent a lot of time putting together a usability document a while back. One high-level goal of the document was just teaching people what usability is and why it's important. However, the document also gets into the deep details of how we use usability at Staples relative to our structure and how it has produced measurable gains. I structured the document so it could be discussed in about an hour, so that it could be scheduled more easily into the calendars of busy senior executives. Some video clips show folks struggling with applications. When

(continued)

*My Nine Principles to Keep
Institutionalization Motivated* (cont.)

somebody says, "What is usability and how does it work?", I use that document to educate them and get the point across.

4. *Speak the language of science, technology, and business.* I think that that's a really important one—it's that "chameleon" idea. You need to be able to go into these people's "dens" and say, "I understand what you're going through. I understand why we can't use Java script on this page, but think about the ROI from a business perspective." You really need to speak in a language they understand. You should not approach it as some Ph.D. scientist in an ivory tower saying, "We should do this because it's right for the user," without really thinking about why it's important to the business or considering it from a technology perspective.

5. *Create a differentiated team.* For example, all my permanent employees and consultants have a master's degree or above in human factors, cognitive psychology, or a related discipline. Many people with great talent in usability do not have these academic credentials. However, having staff with these backgrounds has helped me greatly in selling the usability competency as science throughout the company. Also, I started building the team with the hope that someday we'd move from our original Staples.com roots into other areas of the organization. So I hired folks with backgrounds in retail environments, back-end applications, marketing materials, and paper catalogs. They also had dot-com experience so that until we expanded past dot-com, they would be able to fill the immediate need. As we have grown to support the paper catalog, retail environment, AS-400, and so on, these key folks have been able to grow into other areas of the company.

6. *Tie the group's performance reviews to measurable business metrics.* In the annual performance reviews of my group, I ask them to meet certain measurable criteria. For example, how

are we going to increase the conversion rate or decrease drop-off in Checkout or BizRate Ease of Order survey scores? By tying the group to these metrics, I'm making the statement, "I am a business owner." It helps socialize the idea of usability as a business group. In addition to keeping the usability group focused on business goals, it's a great supplement to having actual profit and loss responsibility.

7. *Work closely with PR to tell the story.* A lot of people may say, "Instead of spending time talking to the media, you should be doing project work." While I agree that spending too much time at conferences and in interviews takes you away from core responsibilities, press coverage has been extremely valuable for us for two reasons. First, it helps get out the positive customer message, which is core to Staples values. Secondly, publicity is extremely valuable in hiring—we have a great PR halo over the usability group. We do good work, but we also talk about the good work that we do. I hope that it helps the usability industry as a whole, but it certainly helps us in hiring. When people say, "Wow, there's a job opening at Staples. Those guys are so focused on usability—I would love to work there," it helps us build a great group.

A couple years ago, I was fortunate enough to take a taxi back from a store to the airport with Tom Stenberg, who was our CEO at the time and is the founder of the office supply superstore concept and of Staples. He said to me, "I read something the other day about the good work your usability team is doing. It must be gratifying to see all the visibility that usability is getting in the press." So when people who are this high up in the organization read the stories, they internalize the ideas. It really helps the internal communication about usability and certainly the external communication about customer focus.

8. *Join professional groups and leverage free advice.* There's lots of free advice out there, from people going through the same

(continued)

My Nine Principles to Keep
Institutionalization Motivated (cont.)

things we are, whether it's SIG CHI, or UPA, or HFES[2] or other groups. There's a lot of good information you can get from picking those brains, and lots of value you can add in return by sharing your own experiences.

9. *Pick your spots.* Speak with passion when necessary—but know when something is good enough. That's a hard thing for a lot of people, especially usability perfectionists. But you need to embrace "good enough." You can't be someone who cries, "Wolf!" all the time. Not everything is the biggest issue to ever happen to the site or the product. You have to keep a sense of perspective. Is this a page that's going to be out there for two days and ten people are going to see it? Or is it something that's going to live with us for years so that millions of people will see it? Pick your spots and don't be a "Chicken Little" whose sky is always falling. It's a basic engineering principle too. "The perfect is the enemy of the good" [Rubinstein and Hersh 1984]—if you try to do everything, you can't get anything done. You have to be a pragmatist.

The level of effort and commitment displayed by the central usability team will pay off in the long term only if team members allow time for maintenance, reinforcement, demonstration, and integration. Together, the team must continue to focus on these goals to keep user-centered design a vital focus of the organization. The final chapter in this book explores the continuing maturity of the usability field.

---

2. The Special Interest Group on Computer-Human Interfaces of the Association for Computing Machinery (SIG CHI), the Usability Professionals Association (UPA), and the Human Factors and Ergonomics Society (HFES).

Chapter 15

The Future

> The field of usability has reached a critical transition point.
> According to Geoffrey Moore's "Crossing the Chasm" paradigm [Moore 1999], usability is ready to become mainstream.
> Usability will follow a maturity path similar to software development and will become an expected attribute of technology products.

Usability is entering a new phase—it is now repeatable. Some fields, such as advertising, by their nature cannot become repeatable. New advertising concepts are a function of artistic magic. While there are certainly better analysis and testing techniques available, the weight of success rides on the unique and often offbeat creative directors. When you select an ad agency, it is in your best interest to know the quality of the creative director assigned to your account.

Usability does have an element of art, but it is primarily an engineering discipline. It is difficult to imagine giving a creative brief to a few different ad agencies and getting the same campaign from all three. It would never happen. But with usability work, it is likely that in the future, you will be able to give a requirements document to three usability companies, and all three will return substantially the same menu or form. Naturally, there will be artistic differences, but the usability principles will be applied systematically, and the menu or form will be easy and repeatable. This is new for our field. We are leaping the chasm from a new technology to a mainstream technology.

Symptoms of Leaping the Chasm

In the past, early adopters applied usability work. In the model of technology adoption created by Geoffrey Moore [1999], usability seems ready to leap the chasm and become the generally accepted approach. Many organizations are engaging in systematic usability efforts, and many more are interested in doing so. Even the most unintelligible applications are touted as "usable" and "easy." So even if the reality is not always present, the motivation is there.

We have seen years of early adoption behavior. Aggressive and visionary managers have completed thousands of isolated usability projects, usually with good results. It is common to encounter organizations that are interested in how to make usability a part of their routine practices. We are on the brink of a mass transition in IT methodology. The foundation in technology is present, and the need is evident. A typical behavior of early adopters is experimentation—and the history of experimentation in usability exists.

In general, when a technology leaps the chasm to widespread usage, a tornado of interest arises. The mass market suddenly wants the technology, and there is not enough of it to go around. There is a bit of frenzy until the market supply meets this demand.

The beginning of this tornado was evident in the later days of the 1990s. The bursting of the dot-com bubble put a damper on the tornado. But we saw a period during which both excellent and weak usability companies were overwhelmed with projects and requests. I predict that the next few years will show a return to this massive interest in usability. I am hopeful that there will be more maturity in the purchasing behavior and that each new usability program will be of good quality and value.

Usability Trends

By Harley Manning, Research Director, Forrester Research

I haven't noticed that people in general are getting smarter. I think what we'll see is the continuation of the old story of the human race, which is that some people will get it, and some people won't.

We do a lot of site reviews—heuristic evaluations—and we meticulously track the scores per question over time and the total scores. This is one way to approximate an average "goodness" number for Web sites of major corporations. And the average score has not been going up in the last four years. Now, this could be a statistical anomaly because even 400 or 500 sites is a small sample. So, part of the analysis is looking at the sites and asking, "Does this look like an improvement to you?" And for the most part, we are still seeing some incredibly basic errors—even at companies that claim to be putting a lot of effort into improving usability.

For example, text legibility is criminal on many sites, just awful. And yet it's so easy to understand what causes poor legibility, and it's so easy to fix it. It costs nothing; it doesn't require you to be a great designer. There's little debate—nobody would argue that it's a good idea to make your customers squint or make it hard to read some marketing communication that you've spent a fortune writing.

So, nobody would argue that poor legibility is a good thing. And very few people are stumped by the fact that increasing type size and increasing foreground/background contrast is the cure for poor legibility. But it doesn't get fixed, and it doesn't get fixed even when you point it out to people.

However, some companies really do get it; they do take usability into account and have very serious efforts. So, while the average Web site is not getting better, there are leaders who really are ahead of the pack and pulling farther ahead.

Maturity

As usability becomes mainstream, it will become integrated. Eventually it will be mature. The maturity of the software industry is something to envy. When coding first began 30 years ago, the programming process was mostly an individual activity. It was completed by unique people who stayed up late and struggled to debug their creations. Their work was a function of flashes of insight and unique, elegant solutions. Yet, in a few decades, the industry has completely changed in character.

The Future of Usability within a Government Agency

**By Sean Wheeler, Lead Usability Specialist,
The Social Security Administration**

I think the recognition of and need for usability services will continue to grow. I believe that as we improve the business case for positive, powerful user experiences and then deliver that kind of experience, the public use of our Web site will increase. This is a critical part of the challenge for agencies like the Social Security Administration if we want more people to choose the information technology channel to contact us.

Quite simply, we must provide a Web experience that meets or exceeds the quality of the experiences that people get when they call our 800 number service or visit their local Social Security office. This was the challenge that our 800 number people faced when we first initiated that service. They had to answer those tough questions about how you communicate that sense of friendliness and provide service on the telephone when you can't see the public visitor face-to-face and share documents with them across a desk. We learned a lot from that channel shift, and we're just now learning what the shift to Web-based service delivery means.

Today, the best software companies have well-documented processes. These companies have defined skill sets and programs to teach their methods to new employees. They have tools and reusable code to make the process faster and more consistent. They know how to accurately estimate and track the effort for a coding project. They assure the quality of their projects, and they continuously improve their process.

Usability will make a similar transformation. It is fun to be unique. But to make usability a part of the business solution, it has to be made more uniform and manageable. Usability has to be systematized. It cannot be the function of luckily having one of the superstars in the field at your disposable. Usability must become institutionalized.

Your Organization's Maturity

There are many dimensions of maturity in usability engineering. Organizations take many different pathways. However, over the years we have discovered typical levels for companies that are climbing the gradient to institutionalized proficiency. Here is one way to look at the path to maturity—based on a model by Earthy [1998].

Level 0: Clueless

In this level, the organization is unaware of usability as a formal discipline. Design is done by intuition and political argument. Any usability effort is directed by a stream of complaints and demands from customers (or worse, from executives or purchasers in a customer's organization).

Level 1: Piecemeal Usability

Here we find early adopters trying to apply usability engineering. There may be training, standards, evaluations, usability testing, and projects of any size. But there is no organizational commitment, and the usability work is not being managed under an overall strategy. The work is not routinely supported by a solid methodology and infrastructure. The effort is not integrated or accepted in the design process. Very good work can happen at this level, but it is still not institutionalization of usability. It is immature.

Level 2: Managed Usability

At this level, the organization has recognized the need for usability as a core capability. An executive champion has created a coherent strategy for usability. Certainly, lots of work still needs to be done. But the usability effort no longer consists of fragmented experiments and good attempts throughout the organization. The usability work is being done as a part of a plan to reach full maturity.

Level 3: Infrastructure

Now the strategy has proceeded to the point where there is a solid infrastructure for usability work. A user-centered methodology has been fit to the organization's development process. There is a reusable template for every deliverable in the methodology and every common questionnaire. A design standard maintains development efficiency and consistency for all the common development environments. Finally, at least one showcase project has proven that these parts work together effectively.

Level 4: Staffing

At this level there is sufficient staff to handle the full set of projects executed by the organization. All projects are supported to an appropriate level (based on their criticality). Generally, we can expect about 10% of the development organization's staff will be usability practitioners. However, this percentage may be a bit different based on the needs of the organization. The staffing can be a composite of consultants, internal staff, and offshore operations.

Level 5: Routine Usability

In this final level, usability has truly been institutionalized. It has become a routine part of the development organization. It is unthinkable that a project would proceed without usability engineering. The usability practitioners are a fully accepted and well-understood part of the design process.

A Vision of the Future of Usability

By Aaron Marcus, President, Aaron Marcus and Associates

I believe that usability groups will try to grow their organization and undertake new initiatives through some of the umbrella developments happening in the corporate world. One of these is the growth of user experience design and user experience engineering. Another growth area is universal design and universal access. A third is cross-cultural usability and the globalization of usability. All of these new concepts lead to new attention and new energy. Whenever paradigms change, it's an appropriate time to move in quickly to obtain additional funding and human resources and to strengthen one's core concerns.

By the way, to clarify: *User experience design* refers to making products and services that are not only usable but also useful and appealing. *Universal design* refers to developing products and services that also meet the needs of the disabled and the elderly. *Globalization* refers to developing products and services that take into account localized needs and desires of a more diverse set of users. Users from different cultures may have very different values for and concepts of power struggles, gender roles, individuality, ambiguity, long-term time orientation, and so on. All of these differences have an impact on what makes products and services usable.

New Technologies

As the information age progresses, the usability field will encounter new challenges. There will be a wave of wearable information appliances, including those that are physically embedded in users (under the skin or in a tooth). Information technology will be applied to new domains and user populations. Each of these domains will present new and interesting challenges. While usability professionals will continue to use the same basic methods and insights, they will have to master some challenging issues.

The usability field will also speed the progress of technology. No longer will we create new offerings only to have them rejected as impractical and awkward. Usability work will soon smooth the introduction of new ideas.

Looking out a decade or two, usability will become so routine it will no longer be a differentiator because all companies will apply a solid process. Today, users do not really clamor for software that calculates correctly. They expect it to work the first time and every time. And if the software does not calculate correctly, they are furious. The same dynamic will occur with usability in the future. Users won't clamor for products that are usable because they will expect them to be usable. And if a product is not usable, they will be furious. The interface quality today will draw derisive laughter from customers in the future. They will expect usability. It will just be one more requirement for being in business.

The time for this transformation, this leaping of the chasm, is now. With a little more work and attention to integrating usability into the organization, we can move the field of usability and, indeed, the quality of the user experience itself, forward.

Appendix

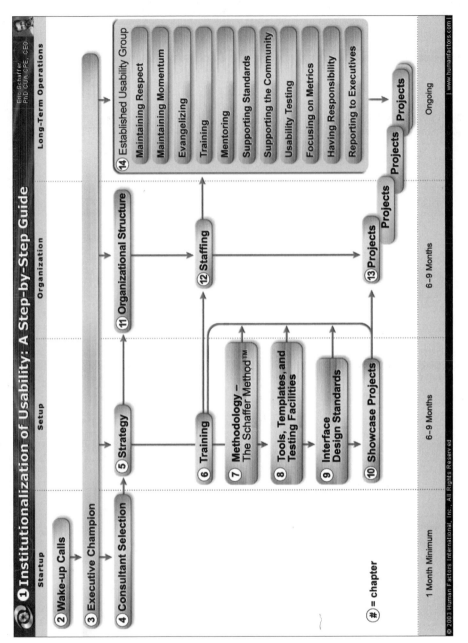

Figure 1-1: *Overview of the Institutionalization of Usability Process*

256

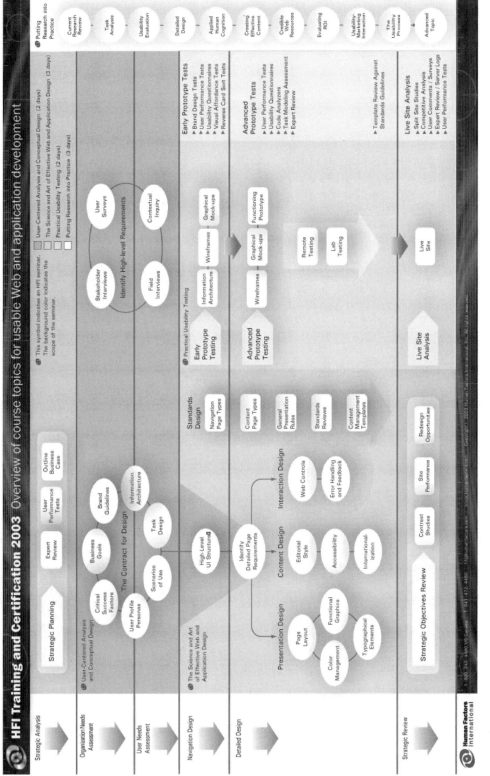

Figure 6-1: *Training Chart: Examples of What Is Taught in Skill Classes to Provide a Solid Level of Training*

257

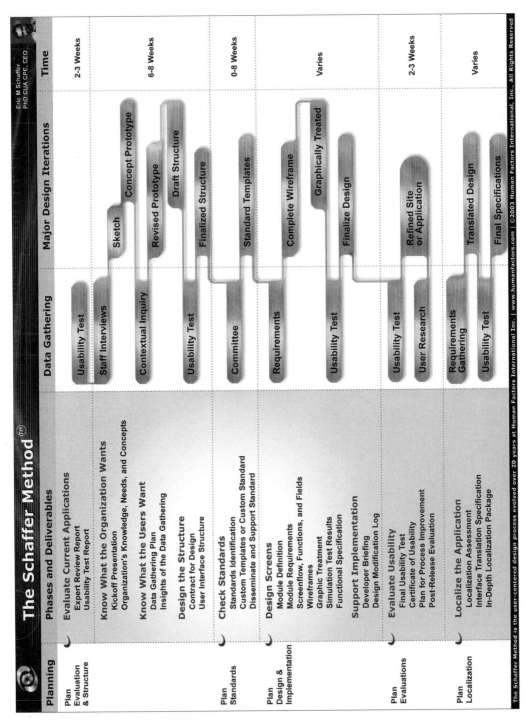

Figure 7-2: *The Schaffer Method*

References

Bernard, Michael. 2002. "Examining User Expectations for the Location of Common E-Commerce Web Objects." *Usability News 4.1.* Accessed in November 2003 at psychology.wichita.edu/surl/usabilitynews/41/web_object-ecom.htm.

Bias, R. G., and D. J. Mayhew 1994. *Cost-Justifying Usability.* San Diego, CA: Academic Press.

Brooks, Frederick P. 1995. *The Mythical Man-Month: Essays on Software Engineering.* Reading, MA: Addison-Wesley.

Card, Stuart K. 1982. "User Perceptual Mechanisms in the Search of Computer Command Menus." In *Proceedings of Human Factors in Computer Systems* (New York: Association for Computing Machinery), 190–196.

Casey, Steven. 1993. *Set Phasers on Stun: And Other True Tales of Design, Technology, and Human Error.* Santa Barbara, CA: Aegean Publishing.

Chavan, Apala L. 2002. "The Bollywood Technique." Unpublished paper presented at User Needs Research Special Interest Group, CHI 2002: Conference on Human Factors in Computing Systems (April 20–25, Minneapolis, MN).

Cooper, Alan. 1999. *The Inmates Are Running the Asylum: Why High-Tech Products Drive Us Crazy and How to Restore the Sanity.* Indianapolis, IN: Sams Publishing.

Earthy, J. 1998. "Usability Maturity Model: Human Centredness Scale." Telematics Applications Project IE 2016, Report from the European Usability Support Centres, WP 5, Deliverable D5.1.4(s),

Version 1.2. Accessed in November 2003 at www.ipo.tue.nl/homepages/mrauterb/lecturenotes/USability-Maturity-Model%5B1%5D.PDF.

Goldberg, Jeff, Geoffrey Montgomery, and Maya Pines. 1995. "Seeing, Hearing and Smelling the World: New Findings Help Scientists Make Sense of Our Senses" (report). Chevy Chase, MD: The Howard Hughes Medical Institute.

Kotelly, Blade. 2003. *The Art and Business of Speech Recognition.* Boston, MA: Addison-Wesley.

Krug, Steve. 2000. *Don't Make Me Think: A Common Sense Approach to Web Usability.* Indianapolis, IN: Que Publishing.

Mayhew, Deborah. 1999. *The Usability Engineering Lifecycle: The Practitioner's Handbook for User Interface Design.* San Francisco: Morgan Kaufmann.

Miller, George A. 1956. "The Magical Number Seven, Plus or Minus Two: Some Limits on Our Capacity for Processing Information." *The Psychological Review,* 63, 81–97.

Moore, Geoffrey. 1999. *Crossing the Chasm: Marketing and Selling High-Tech Products to Mainstream Customers* (rev. ed). New York: HarperBusiness.

Najjar, Lawrence J. 1990. "Using Color Effectively (or Peacocks Can't Fly)" (IBM TR52.0018). Atlanta, GA: IBM Corporation.

Nielsen, Jakob. 1994. *Usability Engineering.* San Francisco: Morgan Kaufmann.

Nielsen, Jakob, and Shuli Gilutz. 2003. *Usability Return on Investment.* Fremont, CA: Nielsen Norman Group.

Nielsen, Jakob, and Marie Tahir. 2001. *Homepage Usability: 50 Websites Deconstructed.* Indianapolis, IN: New Riders Publishing.

Norman, Donald. 2002. "Emotion and Design: Attractive Things Work Better." *Interactions Magazine,* 9(4), 36–42.

———. 1988. *The Design of Everyday Things* (originally published as *The Psychology of Everyday Things*). New York: Basic Books.

Paap, Kenneth R., and Renate J. Roske-Hofstrand. 1986. "The Optimal Number of Menu Options Per Panel." *The Journal of the Human Factors Society*, 28(4), 377–385.

Rehder, Bob, Clayton Lewis, Bob Terwilliger, Peter Polson, and John Rieman. 1995. "A Model of Optimal Exploration and Decision Making in Novel Interfaces." In *Proceedings of CHI Annual Meeting*. Accessed in November 2003 at www.acm.org/sigs/sigchi/chi95/Electronic/documnts/shortppr/br_bdy.htm.

Rubinstein, Richard, and Harry Hersh. 1984. *The Human Factor: Designing Computer Systems for People*. Burlington, MA: Digital Press.

Schaffer, Eric. 2001. "The Institutionalization of Usability" (white paper). Fairfield, IA: Human Factors International.

Schaffer, Eric, John Sorfaten, Glenn Miracle, and Meena Venkateswaran. 1999. "Interactive Voice Response (IVR) Case Study: Testing Your Telephone-Based e-Commerce." *The Journal of Electronic Commerce*, 12(2), 78–84. (Also see www.humanfactors.com/downloads/ivr.asp.)

Schroeder, Will. 1998. "Testing Web Sites with Eye-Tracking." *Eye for Design*, September/October. Accessed in July 2003 at www.uie.com/eyetrack1.htm.

Tinker, Miles A. 1965. *Bases for Effective Reading*. Minneapolis, MN: University of Minnesota Press.

———. 1963. *Legibility of Print*. Ames, IA: Iowa State University Press.

Waite, R. 1982. "Making Information Easy to Use: A Summary of Research." In *Proceedings of International Technical Communication Conference* (Washington, DC: Society for Technical Communication), 120–123.

Ward, Toby. 2001. "Measured Intranet ROI Benefits." *TrendMarkers Newsletter*, 3(7). Accessed in November 2003 at www.techmetrix.com/trendmarkers/publi.php?C=2IOFO.

Index

inform**IT**